How to Love the BIBLE

Derek Allen
C2 Publishing/Mobile

Printed in the United States of America
Second Printing, 2022
ISBN 979-8-218-04437-4

NELLALLEN INC
6508 Sugar Creek Drive South
Mobile, AL 36695

www.howtolovethebible.com

CONTENTS

"It is shallow enough for a child not to drown and deep enough for an elephant to swim." Augustine Speaking of the Gospel of John

Every time I read the Gospel of John, I am amazed by something that I did not see before—every time! What Augustine said about the Gospel of John applies to the entire Bible. God's Word, contained in the 66 books of the Bible is the most complex, intriguing, beautiful, surprising, and inspiring work of art/literature/truth the world has ever known. The only time humanity can be said to have encountered anything like the written Word of God is when Jesus, the Word of God in human flesh, walked the earth. Two thousand years after Jesus took His first breath, the world is still experiencing the impact of His life, death, and resurrection, and 3500 years after the first words of Scripture were written, children are still sharing its waters with elephants.

This book is written to help you dive into the Bible, learn what it teaches, apply its truths to your life, and ultimately develop a deeper love for God and His Word. The academic word for learning to study the Bible is hermeneutics, and in a way, this is a book about hermeneutics. This book, however, was not written with academics in mind. This book was written with those in mind who never had an opportunity to attend a seminary or Bible college, but still have a deep desire to learn about the Bible.

The book presents a process that has been organized around the acronym, BIBLE. I used an acronym for two reasons. First, acronyms are easier to remember. Second, and most importantly, the acronym is a constant reminder for you to follow the process.

The BIBLE Acronym:

B-   Begin with Prayer and Select a Passage
I-   Inspect the Text
B-   Build an Outline
L-   Learn from the Experts
E-   End with Application

My experience is that we are often tempted to start in one of two places. Either we run to learn what the "experts" say by reading commentaries, study Bibles, and articles rather than doing our own personal analysis, or, we pick up the Bible, read some verses, and create our own meanings based on our personal situations. In other words, we apply before we understand.

I believe in the process laid out in this book for three reasons. First, it's based on solid educational and psychological methods. I won't bore you with the details here, but the basic idea is that we learn best when we are challenged, while also being provided with the tools necessary to overcome those challenges. Second, I've taken several groups through this process, and I've witnessed the results. They've learned about passages in the Bible while developing the skills to study the Bible, all at the same time. Third, this is the process I've used for many years, and it has been very helpful for me.

There are so many people to thank for their help with this project. First, I want to thank my assistant, Brooke Wood, and my mother, Kathy Allen, who served as first draft editors for this project. Second, I want to thank the Christ Centered Church family, whose generosity allows me to pastor full-time and practice the craft of writing, and next, I want to thank my wife, Lindsay, for her help with the concept of the book and the design of the cover.

Finally and ultimately, thanks be to God for His Word!
"Oh, the depth of the riches and wisdom and knowledge of God! How unsearchable are his judgments and how inscrutable his ways! 'For who has known the mind of the Lord, or who has been his counselor?' 'Or who has given a gift to him that he might be repaid?' For from him and through him and to him are all things. To him be glory forever. Amen."

1

BEGIN WITH PRAYER AND SELECT A PASSAGE

"It's a dangerous business, Frodo, going out your door. You step onto the road, and if you don't keep your feet, there's no knowing where you might be swept off to." Bilbo Baggins[1]

Consider this the beginning of a journey—a long journey, yes, but not the kind of long journey where you are stuck in the car staring at the back of the seat in front of you for hours on end. This is more like a journey across Europe, or a journey sailing to all the most exotic ports in the world, or, you know, a journey when you leave the shire with a few of your closest hobbit friends headed for the adventure of a lifetime! While this book will not take you on that kind of journey, my hope and aim is that this book will be like a map that leads you deep into another book, the Bible, God's Word, which is more than capable of delivering that kind of journey. Where must this journey begin? It must begin with prayer.

---

[1]. Tolkien, J. R. R. *The Fellowship of the Ring.* Reissue edition. New York: Del Rey, 1986.

BEGIN WITH PRAYER

"When all is said and done, more is said than done." Aesop[2]

It goes without saying that prayer is a vital part of Bible study, but in my experience, much Bible study goes without praying! I have often been guilty of sitting at my desk, opening my Bible, and going right to the task of studying without praying. May the Lord forgive me for being so trite with His Word and prayer. May the Lord bring to our minds the need to pray so that Aesop's words would not be applicable to our prayer lives.

Why Should We Pray?

We all know we *should* pray more, even if we are not sure *why*. So why is prayer so important for Bible study? Here are three reasons:

1. Humility: prayer is one way we confess our dependence on God and remind ourselves of that dependence.
2. Difficulty: Bible study is a difficult task, and we need God's help to be successful.
3. Posture: the Bible is not a dead book. It is living and active, and its Author speaks to us as we read it. That is, of course, if we are listening. Prayer opens our hearts and minds to the voice of God as we read. It's like leaning towards someone telling a great story or sharing really important information so you can hear them more clearly.

When Should We Pray?

I imagine that most of us understand why we should pray when studying the Bible, but we might wonder when to pray. Is it best to pray *before* beginning the process to ask for God's help and blessing as we read? Or is it best to pray *after* we've finished a study session asking God to help us remember and apply what we've learned? Or is it best to pray *as* we study, asking for help in particularly difficult moments or

---

[2].http://www.brainyquote.com/quotes/quotes/a/aesop118961.html

thanking God for insights He gives us? YES! When it comes to Bible study, prayer must be a before, during, and after activity.

What Should We Pray?

Here are a few suggestions for before, during, and after Bible study.

Before:
- Acknowledge God's presence.
- Ask for His help.
- Thank Him for His Word.

During:
- Praise God, through prayer for the beauty and depth of passages as you read and study them.
- Ask God to help you understand specific passages.
- Confess any sinful actions or attitudes in your own life that are being revealed through your study.

After:
- Ask God to write the truth of His Word on your heart.
- Ask for the opportunity to share what you have learned with someone else.
- Ask for the strength to act on what you have learned.

One More Thing about Prayer and Bible Study

Many people are not sure how to pray. Of course, prayer is just a conversation with God, and we can talk to Him just like we would talk to someone who is actually sitting with us. The Lord loves to hear the simple prayers of His children, even when we aren't sure what to say, just like those of us who are parents who love to hear the jumbled words of our babies learning to talk. It's hard to think of something more cute and endearing than baby talk coming from a baby, and it's hard to think of anything more annoying and off-putting than baby talk coming from a full-grown adult!

In other words, we need to let our prayers grow up. Let us follow the example of Paul who said, "When I was a child, I spoke like a child, I thought like a child, I reasoned like a child. When I became a man, I gave up childish ways" 1 Corinthians 13:11. How can we do that? How do we know how to talk to God in a more proper way? We might ask it this way—how can we know how to talk to God in the way God would talk to us? The best way to know how to talk to God is to study the Bible AND allow the Bible to provide the words of our prayers. As you study the Bible, you will find passages that remind you of the goodness, greatness, power, love, grace, mercy, etc. of God. Use the wording of those passages to praise God. For example, read Titus 2:11-14 below, and notice how the prayer written afterwards flows directly from the passage.

> "For the grace of God has appeared, bringing salvation for all people, training us to renounce ungodliness and worldly passions, and to live self-controlled, upright, and godly lives in the present age, waiting for our blessed hope, the appearing of the glory of our great God and Savior Jesus Christ, who gave himself for us to redeem us from all lawlessness and to purify for himself a people for his own possession who are zealous for good works." Titus 2:11-14

> *"Father, thank You for Your grace! You brought salvation to us through Your grace, and You are teaching us to renounce ungodliness and worldly passions. Help me to resist temptation and live a self-controlled, upright, and godly life. Lord, I am waiting for Jesus to appear. He is my hope! He is our great God and Savior! Thank You, Lord for the work of Jesus who gave Himself for me and all those who follow Him. Thank You for redeeming us, purifying us, taking us as Your possession, and giving us a desire to do good works!"*

Often as you study the Bible, you will find passages that are actually written as prayers. Use those to pray for yourself and others. Take a few moments right now and pray for another follower of Christ—maybe someone you have influence over—using Paul's prayer recorded in Ephesians 1:15-19:

> "For this reason, because I have heard of your faith in the Lord Jesus and your love toward all the saints, I do not cease to give thanks for you, remembering you in my prayers, that the God of our Lord Jesus Christ, the Father of glory, may give you the Spirit of wisdom and of revelation in the knowledge of him, having the eyes of your hearts

enlightened, that you may know what is the hope to which he has called you, what are the riches of his glorious inheritance in the saints, and what is the immeasurable greatness of his power toward us who believe."

SELECT A PASSAGE

Studying the Bible is kind of like visiting Disney World—there is so much to see and do that it can be overwhelming to know where to begin or what to do next. Think of this section like those friends we all have who have been to Disney so many times, they know all the ins and outs and even all the secrets. You might not take the advice, but it's worth knowing anyway.

What Are You Interested In?

Why do we encourage children to read books about subjects they like? We know that reading is such an important skill, that children must become good readers to be academically successful, and we know that the best way to become a great reader is to read, and read, and read some more! Putting a book that interests a child in his or her hands is a great way to encourage the child to read. At first, we aren't really concerned about what he reads; we are simply concerned that he learns to read. As my mother, a professional reading coach, often says, "First, children learn to read, then children read to learn."

So, what do you want to know more about? If you want to know about Jesus' life on earth, study the Gospels. If you like poetry, study the Psalms. The topic or book you are interested in most is the best place to start with a few exceptions—don't start in one of the more difficult books or sections. If you don't even know what you would be interested in, the next few pages will help you narrow down potential starting places.

Old Testament or New Testament?

Note: If you are so new to the Bible that you are not even sure what the Old Testament is, then skip this section for now and go to "Where should I start in the New Testament?" If you are aware of the basic Old Testament/New Testament structure, keep reading.

Some people follow this logic:
- Since the Old Testament was written first, and
- Since the New Testament is built upon the Old Testament, and
- Since the first people to read the New Testament did so with the background of the Old Testament in their minds, therefore
- We should begin our study with the Old Testament and work our way towards the New Testament.

Well, maybe so, and maybe not.

The New Testament is not an isolated religious text which stands on its own. I don't mean to say that it doesn't have a message or that we can't learn from it independently of the Old Testament. The gospel is such that it can be understood, believed, and obeyed with the simplest, most basic proclamation. However, as we attempt to explore the depths of the New Testament's message, we will continually come across mysterious caverns, sometimes with the slightest of entrances, which are easily passed over. These contain some of the most glorious spiritual treasures imaginable, and over those caverns are chiseled the names of the 39 books constituting the Hebrew Scriptures of the Old Testament.

So should we start with the Old Testament in order to get the foundation needed to understand the New Testament? Not in my opinion, and let me emphasize that this is just an opinion. There is no clear direction in Scripture on where we should start our study of Scripture, and there are many different ways to approach this question.

To understand my point of view, think of the Old Testament like the foundation of a tall, beautiful building. If we want to study the architecture and engineering of that building, we need to study and understand the design of the foundation buried deep into the bedrock which supports the more visible and accessible sections of the building. Otherwise, our understanding of the building's design will remain partial and somewhat surface level. That does not mean, however, that we should or must study the foundation first. In fact, it would be very odd to visit a beautiful building and go directly to the basement to see the supporting columns. Walk through the front door! Admire the layout, design, and artwork of the foyer. Ride the elevator to the observatory and take in the 360-degree view of the city. Then, once you are amazed at the building as-is, complete and presented in the way it was intended by its designer, pull out the blueprints and start to study the design.

Where Should I Start in the New Testament?

Now that we've narrowed the starting point down considerably (the New Testament contains less than 25% of the words in the Bible), how do we choose our starting point? Using the building illustration from above, where is the front door to the building? Let me suggest the Gospels, specifically the Synoptic Gospels.

The Synoptic Gospels are Matthew, Mark, and Luke, and if you follow the method of this book, it doesn't really matter which one of those three you choose. They are called the Synoptics, because they see (optics) from the same (syn) viewpoint—they tell the same basic story. Studying one requires comparing it with the other two as you go, so you end up studying all three. My suggestion is that you study Mark because 1) most scholars believe it was written before the other two, and 2) it is the shortest of the three.

What's Next?

Maybe you've just finished studying a Synoptic Gospel or maybe you grew up in church, and you feel like you've been looking around the foyer of the building for so long that you're ready for a different view. A Pauline Epistle would be a great place to explore next. The Pauline Epistles are the books of the New Testament written by the Apostle Paul, which begin with Romans and end with Philemon.

As you study the Pauline Epistles, here are a few pointers:
- Don't start with Romans. Yes, it is the height of Pauline and perhaps biblical thought, but so is Mount Everest, the height of the earth's crust, and only fools climb Everest first!
- Start with 1 Corinthians, 2 Corinthians, Galatians, Ephesians, Philippians, Colossians, 1 Thessalonians, or 2 Thessalonians since those books are written to churches and not individuals.
- When you decide to study Romans, consider doing so one section at a time (chapters 1-6, then chapters 7-11, then 12-16) and studying other books or passages between. This will help you digest and absorb the message of the book in manageable pieces.

Continue to vary your diet to include a balance of Synoptic Gospels, Pauline Epistles, the Gospel of John, General Epistles (James-Revelation), and books from the Old Testament. The same warning which applied to Romans applies to Hebrews and Revelation as well. Enjoy them, but develop your study skills elsewhere before striking out to climb these giants.

Which Book in the Old Testament?

Studying the Old Testament can be one of the most enriching and surprising journeys a follower of Christ will ever take. Many who want to study the Old Testament, however, have no idea where to start. Before recommending an order, first let me explain the sections of the Old Testament—there are five.

Five Sections of the Old Testament
The Old Testament is not arranged chronologically, but by genre, or type of writing.

The Books of Moses. The first five books of the Bible (Genesis, Exodus, Leviticus, Numbers, and Deuteronomy) were written by Moses and are often called the Torah or the Pentateuch.

History Books. Starting with Joshua and extending through Esther, these books pick up the history of Israel after Moses' death and continue to tell the story through the fall of Israel, her exile, and her return to the Promised Land.

Wisdom Literature. The books from Job to Song of Solomon are known as wisdom literature. They are sometimes called the poetic books, and they contain a wide variety of writing styles and genres.

Major Prophets. Isaiah, Jeremiah, Lamentations, Ezekiel, and Daniel are some of the longest books in the entire Bible and record words of prophecy which span several hundred years of Jewish history.

Minor Prophets. The twelve books from Hosea to Malachi are often called the Minor Prophets, not because they are less important than the Major Prophets, but because they are shorter and generally cover a shorter time period. In the Jewish Scriptures, they are combined into one book called the Book of the Twelve.

Choosing a Starting Place

When it comes to the books of the Old Testament, it's probably just as important to say where you *shouldn't* start! Don't start with Leviticus, Ecclesiastes, Lamentations, Ezekiel, or Zechariah. While these are all incredibly relevant books with important messages, in my opinion, their genre (style of writing) or the historical background of the reader makes them very difficult to approach for new students of the Bible.

I suggest that those who want to study the Old Testament begin with some of the great narrative sections. Narratives tell stories, and we love stories. Genesis, Exodus 1-20, Judges, Ruth, 1 and 2 Samuel, 1 and 2 Kings, and Esther each contain surprising, challenging, easy to understand (mostly!) narratives. One powerful feature of these narratives is that many of us who grew up going to Sunday School think we know these stories and then, as we read and study them for ourselves, we are shocked by what we didn't know about so many familiar stories.

Once you've studied some of the great narratives of the Old Testament, I suggest studying one of the Minor Prophets (other than Zechariah). These books are shorter and normally address one central issue. Many of them have a time stamp in the first verse that allows the reader to easily study the background of the book, and they contain memorable images that, once understood, communicate powerful truths about God and His relationship with His people.

Once you've honed your study skills in the narratives and Minor Prophets, you will be ready to study any section of the Old Testament.

Table 1 combines the information above and suggests an order to follow. It's designed so you can start at any place, move from left to right, line by line, and maintain a healthy, balanced diet of Bible study.

More Advanced Methods for Choosing Books or Passages

Those who have studied Scripture for many years and are looking for a more challenging and rewarding approach, consider one of the following methods:

- Study one of the more difficult books of the New Testament (Romans, Hebrews, or Revelation).

Table 1: Suggested Reading Plan

	Synoptic Gospel	Pauline Epistle	OT Book	Gospel of John or Acts	General Epistle	OT Book
#1	Mark	Ephesians	Genesis	John	James	Ruth
#2	Matthew	Galatians	Amos	Acts 1-7	1 John	Exodus 1-20
#3	Luke	1 Corinthians	Habakkuk	John 1-12	1 Peter	Judges
#4	Mark	1 Timothy	Daniel	Acts 8-11	2 Peter	1&2 Samuel
#5	Matthew	Colossians	1&2 Kings	John 13-22	2&3 John	Jeremiah
#6	Luke	Philippians	Lamentations	Acts 13-28	Jude	Ecclesiastes

- Study one of the more difficult books of the Old Testament (Leviticus, Isaiah, Ezekiel or, Zechariah).
- Study the books of either the Old Testament or the New Testament in chronological order. A simple Internet search will provide a chronological list—be aware that scholars often disagree about chronology, but don't get too caught up in that debate. Just pick a list from a reliable source and start studying.
- Study all the New Testament books written by one author. John, Luke, Paul, and Peter all wrote multiple books in the New Testament, and studying them together reveals nuances of each author's theology and message.
- Study characters or concepts. Study all the passages that discuss Abraham, David, Solomon, John, Barnabas, Timothy, etc. or how concepts such as forgiveness or atonement develop from Genesis through Revelation.
- Study the New Testament's use of the Old Testament. The New Testament quotes and alludes to the Old Testament more than most of us realize, and studying which passages are used and how the New Testament authors use them can really enrich our understanding of God and His Word.
- Study the great doctrines of the Bible like the doctrines of sin, humanity, salvation, God's triune nature, or the nature of Scripture.

How Much Should I Study at One Time?

That's like asking how much food someone should eat—the simple answer is, as much as you can handle, enjoy and process in a healthy way. There is no magic word count, verse count, or chapter count. My suggestion is that you take the process chapter-by-chapter, verse-by-verse, or even word-by-word if necessary, until you understand the message. This is a treasure hunt, not a money grab. There is enough in Scripture for you to enjoy for a lifetime, and the longer you stay in one section, the more you will receive from that section. 'But I've got to read through the Bible in a year!' Who said so?

It seems odd to think that we might spend our entire lives studying one book and never exhaust all of our study options, but when it comes to Scripture, it's true. The Bible is as inexhaustible as its Author. In fact, those who study the Bible at the highest levels grow to realize, with each new discovery, how many truths lay just beyond the next horizon, and the next, and the next . . . until that day comes when they place their eyes on a horizon too far in the distance for the strength and time left in their life on this earth. It's that realization that gives rise to the conviction that Heaven is not simply a place for those who would prefer not to go to Hell, but rather it is a place for those who, through the message of the gospel and study of the Word, have developed a hunger for God, which could not be fully satisfied in 10,000 lifetimes.

Conclusion

It's impossible to study the Bible without selecting a passage, and it's unfruitful to study the Bible unless you begin, continue, and end with prayer. Now that we've laid the foundation, in the following chapters, we will learn how to Inspect the Text, Build an Outline, Learn from the Experts, and End with Application.

Learn to Love the **BIBLE**:

B-Begin with Prayer and Select a Passage
I-
B-
L-
E-

Next Steps

1. Prayerfully select a passage to study as you learn the BIBLE process.
2. Write out a prayer asking the Lord to help you learn to love Him and know Him on a deeper level through studying the passage you've selected.
3. Text or email two friends asking them to stop whatever they are doing to pray for you as you begin this process.

2

INSPECT THE TEXT PART 1

"The key to good exegesis, and therefore to a more intelligent reading of the Bible, is to learn to read the text carefully and to ask the right questions of the text." Gordon D. Fee and Douglas Stuart[3]

If you grew up in the 1980's, then you probably strapped a towel around your head at some point and pretended to be the Karate Kid. The 1984 iconic movie featured a young man named Daniel who was transformed into a karate champion by the unconventional training methods of Mr. Miyagi, the maintenance man at Daniel's apartment complex, who also happened to be a world class martial artist.

The early stages of Daniel's training with Mr. Miyagi were frustrating, because he spent hours washing and waxing Mr. Miyagi's car, as well as painting his fence. If you've seen the movie, then you most certainly remember, "Wax on. Wax off." As the story progresses, Daniel comes to understand that Miyagi used those seemingly menial tasks to teach him all the basic moves needed in training. In other words, because Daniel trusted Miyagi and didn't give up when the methods didn't seem to make sense, Daniel became a karate champion.

---

[3]. How to Read the Bible for All Its Worth, 26

I'm not Mr. Miyagi, and I'd bet most of you aren't on your way to any karate championships either, but, if you are serious about learning to study the Bible, then I'm asking you to trust me and stick with the process described in the next few chapters. There will be times when the tasks may seem menial, but they have a purpose, and skipping any of them will undermine the entire method.

So, what's first? Once you've selected a text, the next step is inspecting the text, and inspecting the text starts with reading the text.

Read

Start by reading the text you are studying in at least three different translations (versions of the Bible). Before explaining this process in more detail, let me emphasize a very important point—you should choose one translation as your primary translation for studying. For help choosing a translation, or if you are really confused about all the different versions and translations of the Bible, see the APPENDIX 1. So, read the passage in two or more translations in addition to the regular Bible you use for study.

Reading multiple translations is helpful for several reasons. First, there are stylistic differences between translations, and one translation might make the message of the passage click with you more than other versions. This is especially true if you have been exposed to one translation more than others. Simply reading a familiar passage in a different translation can often make that passage come alive in a new way.

Second, most major disputes among scholars about the meaning of the Greek or Hebrew words or phrases behind the English text become evident when translations are compared. Third, reading the text multiple times saturates our minds with the Word of God.

The most important factor in choosing which translations to read is variety. That doesn't mean you should choose different translations each time. In fact, it's not a bad idea to always read the same three or four translations each time you study. By variety, I mean you should choose translations from different categories or types of translations.

Table 2 categorizes translations according to factors such as source manuscripts, translation philosophy, and readability, and in most cases, you should read at least one translation from groups 1, 2, and 3. Group 4, the paraphrases, can be helpful for more difficult passages, but paraphrases often move far away from what the original text actually says, and they should be read with a hint of suspicion. For more information about these factors or translations in general, see APPENDIX 1. Table 3 lists 2 Corinthians 8:1 in one translation from each group.

Table 2: Bible Translations by Category

Group 1 (Textus Receptus)	Group 2 (Formal Equivalence)	Group 3 (Dynamic Equivalence)	Group 4 (Paraphrase)
King James Version	English Standard Version	New International Version	New Living Translation
New King James Version	New American Standard Bible	Holman Christian Standard Bible	The Living Bible
Young's Literal Translation	Mounce Reverse-Interlinear NT		The Message

Table 3: 2 Corinthians 8:1 In Four Translations

Group 1 (King James)	Group 2 (English Standard)	Group 3 (New International)	Group 4 (The Message)
"Moreover, brethren, we do you to wit of the grace of God bestowed on the churches of Macedonia."	"We want you to know, brothers, about the grace of God that has been given among the churches of Macedonia."	"And now, brothers and sisters, we want you to know about the grace that God has given the Macedonian churches."	"Now, friends, I want to report on the surprising and generous ways in which God is working in the churches in Macedonia province."

Notice how each translation has a different feel. Also, notice how each one says basically the same thing, but they all have different ways of saying it. Reading various translations of a passage is like reading a math sentence written several different ways. Two plus two is four. 2+2=4. The sum of two and two is four. Two twos make one four. Each one communicates the same information, but one format might be more helpful for a particular student than another. Exposing your mind to different formats, or translations, of a Scripture passage, will help you better understand the passage.

List Questions

As you read, questions will naturally arise, and you should write them down, no matter how insignificant they might seem. Which questions are relevant and important? At this stage, there's no way you can know that, so write them all down. This is THE MOST VITAL PART of the Inspect the Text step. In fact, it is so important that I want to give examples of questions from 2 Corinthians 8:1.

- Why did Paul say "We want you to know" and not "I want you to know?"
- What does the term "brothers" (ESV) mean?
- What is the "grace of God that has been given?" Is that the grace involved in salvation or something else?
- What is grace?
- Why is "churches" plural and not singular?
- Where is Macedonia?
- Why is Paul talking about churches from Macedonia when he is writing to the church at Corinth?

Now it's your turn. Read 2 Corinthians 8:9 below, and make a list of questions. And yes, I'm serious—take a short break from reading and make a list of questions. "But what if I ask questions that don't really even make sense?" You probably will, and that's okay. You aren't turning these questions into anyone!

> "For you know the grace of our Lord Jesus Christ, that though he was rich, yet for your sake he became poor, so that you by his poverty might become rich."

How did you do? As long as you listed a few questions, you did great. The point is not to ask profound questions, but rather to ask your questions. You might wonder, "How will I know if I'm asking the right questions?" In the next chapter, I will give you some specific questions to ask of every passage you study, but it's more important that you start with your questions than the "right" questions. Why? Because your questions indicate what has piqued your curiosity about the text.

These questions, the ones that you naturally ask as you read the text carefully, will become the windows through which you study and understand the passage. Let me give you an example. When I first studied 1 Corinthians 8, I was curious about the phrase in verse 1, "the grace of God that has been given among the churches of Macedonia." The rest of chapter 8 discusses a financial gift given from the churches in Macedonia to the churches in Jerusalem. So, I wondered, why does Paul describe a gift from one group of people to another as the grace of God? Furthermore, why does Paul say that this gift, which he describes as the grace of God, was given among the churches of Macedonia and not from the churches of Macedonia or to the churches in Jerusalem? While there are many important phrases in that chapter, that one phrase became the lens through which I understood the entire passage. Because it made me curious, when I found a satisfactory answer, I grasped the principle in a way that impacted me deeply.

Professional rock climbers amaze me. They can scale a seemingly smooth rock face as though it has a ladder attached. When I tried climbing myself, I learned how important it is to gain a foothold. Once you have a foot solidly set, it's much easier to examine the options for your next move and determine a path to climb the rock. The same is true with understanding a passage. At first, it doesn't really matter which part of the passage you understand; what matters is that you gain a foothold of understanding somewhere in the passage. From a solid foothold, you can navigate your way to understanding other parts of the passage. Your curiosity is likely to guide you to a great foothold, not because your curiosity is keenly attuned to ask the best questions, but because your curiosity will keep you searching until you find a foothold.

Once, a friend and I were studying the first chapter of the Gospel of John together. The Gospel of John is named after its author, John the Apostle, the brother of James. Another man named John, John the Baptist, plays an important role in the first chapter. As my friend and I read the passages about John the Baptist, he was curious. He asked, "Why is John talking about himself so much?" Of course, my friend, a new student of the Bible, did not know that John, the author of the book, and John the Baptist were different people. Once I explained that to him, he understood, but he also learned something else. As we walked through the Gospel of John, he learned that the author, John the Apostle, never mentions himself by name, and that has significant theological importance. The point is, my friend found a foothold by asking a question. He was curious about the way John wrote about himself. That question, even though it was based on an illegitimate observation, led to a foothold that helped him explore the passage and book.

Make Observations

Observations are different from questions, but the process is very similar. Basically, an observation is any conclusion you can draw from a verse no matter how insignificant it seems. Here's an example of observations from 2 Corinthians 8:1.

- Paul cares about what the church at Corinth knows.
- Knowledge is important.
- We can know about God's grace.
- The early churches knew about each other.
- God's grace can be given in such a way that it can be described as being given corporately (to a group).
- There were multiple churches in Macedonia.

Depending on your level of background knowledge and experience, you might be able to list many more observations, and you should challenge yourself to make more and more observations as you grow in knowledge and ability. Table 4 suggests the number of observations you should look for per verse based on level of difficulty and the length of the passage.

So, if you are just getting started (beginner level), and you are studying three verses, you should try to find one observation per verse. If you've been studying the Bible for a long time, want to study at more in-depth levels (or if you just want a challenge!), and you are studying a passage with five verses, you should try to make ten observations per verse. If you're intimidated by the most difficult level, but not challenged by the lowest levels, then try level 3. In that case, if you study a passage with twelve verses, then your goal is to make three observations per verse.

Table 4: Number of Observations

# of Verses in Passage	Observations at Desired Level of Difficulty (1-Beginner, 5-Expert)				
	1	2	3	4	5
1-5	1	3	5	7	10
6-15	1	1	3	5	7
16-30	Choose a Shorter Passage	1	1	3	5
31-50	Choose a Shorter Passage	Choose a Shorter Passage	1	1	3
50+	Choose a Shorter Passage	Choose a Shorter Passage	Choose a Shorter Passage	1	1

Now it's your turn again. Read 2 Corinthians 8:9, and try to list at least three observations from the verse.

> *"For you know the grace of our Lord Jesus Christ, that though he was rich, yet for your sake he became poor, so that you by his poverty might become rich."*

Don't focus on deep, profound observations—just write down what you see as plainly taught in the verses you are studying. Whatever you do, at this stage, don't use a commentary, a study Bible, or even an Internet search to find observations. Just read the text and look for plainly taught truths. Many people make the mistake of looking for some kind of encoded meaning in the Bible, when the real meaning— the one God intended for us to know and live by—is the straightforward meaning. In other words, the Bible says what it means and means what it says.

How did you do? Making observations is a skill that will grow as you use it, and you should challenge yourself to make more and more observations per verse as you grow in your Bible study skills. When it comes to observations, remember two rules of thumb:

- Quantity over quality—every legitimate observation made about a Scripture passage is valuable, so make as many observations as you can. Sometimes the most profound truths are also the simplest truths, and if you spend all your time looking for something tweetable, you will likely miss the simple, profound, and life changing truths.
- If it's new, it's not true—godly scholars have studied every passage of the Bible for two millennia and more. It's not likely, better yet, not possible, that you and I will be the first to stumble upon a profound truth that all of the church churches and the Jewish scholars before them have missed. As we make observations, therefore, we must be properly cautious before running to the town square and proclaiming these truths for all to hear. We will hold them in our minds, yes, but we must wait and see if they stand the test of rigorous evaluation and further study.

In 1828, gold was discovered in the mountains of North Georgia and a gold rush ensued. Like other gold rushes, the first wave of miners found it easy to gather the gold. Some reported nuggets of gold just lying uncovered on the ground. Others dredged the bottom of streams where gold had settled as it was washed off the mountainside. Then, after the easy gold was mostly gone, miners started digging into the mountains looking for gold deposits, called veins. These deposits were often deep into the side of the mountain and had to be chiseled out of hard rock, taken to the surface, and crushed in a mill in order to extract the gold. While mining for deposits was harder work, finding a good deposit was worth the effort because it produced larger amounts of gold.

Imagine being one of those first miners who found the gold when it was so abundant and undisturbed that it was just lying around on the surface. The Bible is full of that kind of treasure, and no matter how many people have discovered it before us, there it is, still lying on the ground for us to discover all over again, but under the surface are deep, rich deposits that are worth all the hard work required to access them. While it's unlikely, it's not impossible, that we will ever find a deposit which hasn't been discovered or mined before;, for every new Bible student, each deposit waits to be discovered all over again, in all its beauty, value, and excitement for those willing to put in the work.

Conclusion

Begin with Prayer, Select a Passage, and Inspect the Text. These foundational steps will prepare you spiritually and mentally for understanding the meaning and identifying proper implications and applications of Bible passages. In this chapter, we've discussed the first steps in the process of inspecting the text—reading, asking questions, and making observations. As you take these steps, the learning process will begin, and the meaning of the passage will start to become clear. Really, however, these steps are just preparatory, like sanding wood before painting it. Follow the process, and by the time you are finished, what you've learned will stick!

Learn to Love the BIBLE:

B-Begin with Prayer and Select a Passage
I- Inspect the Text:
        Read
        List Questions
        Make Observations
B-
L-
E-

Next Steps

1. Read and re-read your selected passage, praying for wisdom and insight as you read.
2. Decide where and how you will take notes (computer, phone, journal, notebook) and list the questions you have as you read the passage.
3. Using Table 4 in this chapter, set a goal for the number of observations per verse, and record your observations.

3

INSPECT THE TEXT PART 2

"The ability to ask the right question is more than half the battle of finding the answer." Thomas J. Watson[4]

I love to play basketball. At some point in my life, basketball bordered on an unhealthy addiction, so you can understand my response to the coach of our high school team. It was just after tryouts, and my coach called me into his office. "It's like this," he said, "I need 10 players, and you're number 11. I'm going to leave the decision up to you, but if you stay on the team, you need to know that you probably won't get to play in any games." What did I say? YES! I loved to play so much that going to practice was enough for me.

Practice is different from playing in the driveway. In the driveway, you pick up a ball, bounce it, shoot it, and just see what happens. At practice, however, someone who knows about basketball gives instruction and hones specific skills, which lead to success on the court. So far, we've been playing in the driveway, and that's important, but now it's time to hone our skills.

---

[4]. Thomas John Watson, Sr.: http://www.quotes.net/quote/18769.

Now that you've "played in the driveway" and are armed with a list of questions and observations that may or may not be correct, what's next? Asking more questions and making more observations! Only this time, you need to take a more guided approach.

Question the Text

Although there is some overlap, this is different from listing the questions that arise as you read the text. That's more passive, like a visitor to Lincoln Memorial in Washington who notices that Lincoln faces the National Mall and wonders why. Questioning the text is more active—like a skilled lawyer carefully asking questions of a witness to extract specific information.

Who, What, When, Where, Why, and How

How exactly, then do we question the text? I'm glad you asked. Journalists use the basic questions of who, what, when, where, why, and how to understand the details of a story, and we can use those questions to ask relevant questions of verses and entire passages. By "relevant questions," I mean those questions that make sense, given the verse or passage.

For example, let's return to 2 Corinthians 8:9, and ask each question.

> *"For you know the grace of our Lord Jesus Christ, that though he was rich, yet for your sake he became poor, so that you by his poverty might become rich."*

- Who? The Lord Jesus Christ
- What? He was rich and became poor
- When? The verse does not answer that question
- Why? For the sake of His followers—that they might become rich
- How? This is somewhat an irrelevant question. It seems to be answered by the other information drawn out by the previous questions.

I've found that everyone applies these questions differently. For instance, some might answer the "Who?" question from the perspective of those being saved rather than the perspective of the one doing the saving. So, instead of saying, "The Lord Jesus Christ" as I did, they might say, "You (the church at Corinth)." Neither answer is wrong; they just represent different perspectives, and they require the other questions to be answered differently.

Important Reminders When Asking the Reporter Questions:
- Ask the reporter questions of each paragraph, section, or set of verses.
- Not every question will apply to every passage or section.
- Use the question or questions that apply most directly to the section you are questioning.
- Answer any of the questions you can and include them in your list of observations.
- When studying several verses, ask the questions of larger sections, and look for less detailed answers.
- When studying a few verses, dig in and look for more specific details.

Asking the reporter questions will create additional observations for your list, and it will likely generate questions you can't answer, which you can add to your list of questions. The point is not to understand all the who, what, when, where, why, and how of a passage; the point is to struggle and wrestle with the text so the text works itself deep into your heart and mind.

Questions about the Original Languages

The Bible was originally written in ancient Hebrew (Old Testament) and a type of ancient Greek often called Koine Greek[5] (New Testament) with a few sections of the Old Testament and a few words in the New Testament written in Aramaic. Anytime one language is translated to another, some of the meaning gets lost, so studying the original languages of the Bible can be very helpful. If you are just starting to study the Bible, this might be a skill you want to develop later, but if you're ready now, this section will help you begin. Don't

---

[5]. Koine Greek is a type of Greek language that developed in the first century BC and was used during the 1st century AD. It is less formal than the classical Greek of Plato, Homer, etc.

worry, there's no need to be a language scholar or to even know how to read Greek or Hebrew.

Two Approaches

There are two ways to study the Hebrew and Greek texts[6] behind the English translations. The first approach begins with the Hebrew and Greek texts and translates every word. While that approach is more thorough, it is also more time consuming and requires a significant level of expertise in those languages. The second approach is to start with the English text and only study the Hebrew and Greek words and phrases, which are significantly different from their English translations; that's the approach outlined in this section.

Unless you want to be a Hebrew or Greek scholar, why would you spend time trying to learn the meaning of Hebrew and Greek words? Those words have already been translated into English words that very accurately communicate their original meanings. Wouldn't it be better to only study the words whose meanings aren't clearly represented by the English words or phrases used to translate them? Wouldn't it be nice if there was a way to know which words or phrases might not be clearly represented by their English translations? Yes. Good news! There is a simple way to identify those words and phrases.[7]

To identify the words and phrases that will be most beneficial for study in the original languages, carefully compare English translations with each other. Doing so will identify translation issues that scholars struggle to solve. Such issues end up translated differently across different versions of the Bible. Once again, consider 2 Corinthians 8:1.

The Message paraphrase has been removed from this table because it does not attempt to translate the words of the original languages directly, so it is not helpful in this kind of discussion. Notice how many subtle but important differences occur among these translations.

---

[6]. Since only a small section of the Bible is written in Aramaic, we will focus our attention on how to learn about the Greek and Hebrew texts. Many of the principles also apply to the study of the Aramaic sections.

[7]. Even though the approach described here will be very helpful, the best way to study the Bible in its original languages is to learn those languages! If you have the time and ability to learn Greek and/or Hebrew, it will greatly enhance your understanding of the message of the Bible.

Should we understand Paul's words as written to brothers, brethren, or brothers and sisters? Was the grace of God given to, given among, or bestowed upon the Macedonian churches? Is there an "And" at the beginning of the verse? Which phrase comes first, "We want you to know," or an address to the "brothers/brethren/brothers and sisters?"

Group 1 (King James)	Group 2 (English Standard)	Group 3 (New International)
"Moreover, brethren, we do you to wit of the grace of God bestowed on the churches of Macedonia."	"We want you to know, brothers, about the grace of God that has been given among the churches of Macedonia."	"And now, brothers and sisters, we want you to know about the grace that God has given the Macedonian churches."

Now that we've identified several differences in English translations, let's choose a few to study further using the original language, which in this case, is Greek. The two issues that seem most significant to the meaning of the text are whether it was written to brothers (brethren) or brothers and sisters and whether the grace of God was given to, given among, or bestowed upon the Macedonian churches. Now it's time to use a very helpful tool called Blue Letter Bible.

Use Blue Letter Bible to Explore the Greek Words of 2 Corinthians 8:1:
1. Go to www.blueletterbible.org.
2. Type, 2 Corinthians 8:1 in the "Search the Bible" box.
3. Click on the dark blue text which says 2Co 8:1.
4. A box with several tools will appear, and one of tools will be labeled 'Interlinear'. If it's not already highlighted, click on it.
5. Inside the interlinear tool, each English word is listed along with the Greek word from the original text. Each word also has a number under the heading Strong's. Find the word "brothers" or "brethren" and click on the Strong's number (in this case, it's 80).
6. Many resources appear for the word, adelphos, which is the Greek word translated brothers, brethren, and brothers and sisters in the three English translations above. Explore those resources to learn more about the word.

What did you learn? According to the sources at Blue Letter Bible, adelphos literally means brothers. It comes from two words which mean of the same womb. However, the word also came to be used to mean people, both male and female, belonging to the same community, and even more specifically, Christians belonging to the same community. So, it's easy to understand why the translators aren't sure if they should use the literal meaning (brothers/brethren) or the implied meaning (people of both sexes in the Christian community at Corinth, or brothers and sisters). Regardless of the translators' reasons for making their decisions, your careful study of this word has now helped you understand it more deeply. Christians are in such close community to one another that we can be described as those connected to the same womb!

Now, using the same steps above, research the word or phrase translated given to, given among, or bestowed upon. What did you find?

As we take this approach to studying languages, we will find little significance to some of the translation differences, but others will make a big difference in the meaning of the verse and the verses that follow. By completing this process, you will be better prepared to interact with the scholarly sources that will be consulted later.

Conclusion

Imagine a basketball coach bringing in his team each day, seating them in the bleachers and then marvelously executing passing drills, dribbling drills, and shooting drills while the players watch. Imagine that same coach calling a friend who played professional basketball to come and lecture the players about technique and strategy and then show the players a few of his skills. That's no way to teach people how to play basketball. Information and examples are great, but they will only be helpful as supplements of actual, hands-on practice. Of course the coach and his friend are better at basketball, and of course the players will not be that great at first. If they never pick up a ball, they will never learn!

Many of you have spent years listening to sermons, and that hasn't made you a great student of the Bible—it has helped, for sure, but its effects are limited. Others have read the organized thoughts of those who have studied the Bible, and that has helped as well. However, if you never pick up the Bible, just the Bible, and struggle with a text to find its meaning, implications, and applications, then you will never learn how to study the Bible. You will always need someone else to process and package it for you.

The goal when inspecting the text—making observations, listing questions, questioning the text—is not to find all the right answers, but to familiarize ourselves with the text and the interpretive issues of the text. We are examining and struggling with the text. In fact, at this stage, if a student has more questions than answers, or if he or she has no answers at all, then the student is prepared to learn. Like a house which has been scraped and sanded is prepared for a new coat of paint, a student with more questions than answers is prepared to learn in a way that will stick!

Learn to Love the **BIBLE**:

B-Begin with Prayer and Select a Passage
I- Inspect the Text:
      Read
      List Questions
      Make Observations
      Question the Text
B-
L-
E-

Next Steps

1. Read your selected passage again, asking who, what, when, where, why, and how.
2. Record your answers, and if the answer is not clear from the text, add the question to your list of questions. Remember that all six questions will rarely make sense for a passage, so only use the relevant questions.
3. If you're ready to try studying the original languages, compare translations again and look for significant differences, use blueletterbible.org or a similar resource and record your observations.
4. Pray that the Lord will write His Word on your heart.

4

INSPECT THE TEXT PART 3

The website Out of Context Quotes[8] catalogs lines from popular culture, which make no sense outside of the conversation in which they originally occurred. Here are a few:

"Even brain surgery is easier when you're a professional chef!"
"T-Rex will never know the joy of putting olives on the end of his claws."
"Since the angels got out of the bathroom, they've been very crunchy."
"Everything with you revolves around opposable thumbs."
"Fish Licking is frowned upon, especially in New England."

Yes, it's okay to laugh while reading a book about studying the Bible. While these quotes make me smile, they also make me really curious about the kind of conversation in which these lines would make sense. Every conversation, every work of literature, and every written and spoken word has a literary context. The passages of the Bible are no exception.

CONSIDER THE LITERARY CONTEXT

"You're taking that out of context!" That phrase has been used so often and applied so universally to any interpretive error that it is in danger of losing any actual meaning. Nevertheless, the word "context"

---

[8]. http://www.outofcontextquotes.com/wordpress/

simply means that which is with (con) a text, and to understand a biblical passage, we must understand it in its context.

Each passage has an immediate context, a larger context, and a historical context. Let me illustrate. In just a moment, I want you to close your eyes and imagine you hear the word "FIRE" yelled loudly, and imagine what's going on around you. Go ahead. I'll wait. . . Ok, what did you imagine? Let me give you some context. The immediate context is that the person who yelled the word is picking a football up off the ground. The larger context is that you are playing a football game, and that man is the place holder for your football team; the historical context is that your coach has trained the team to know that the word "FIRE" is the signal that the snap has been fumbled and all the receivers should go out for a pass. Did any of you imagine that scenario? Now, even if you don't know anything about football, you can recognize the point—context determines meaning.

One passage which is often heard out of context is Matthew 7:1, "Judge not, that you be not judged." That's very clear—if you judge others, you will be judged by God, so it's wrong to tell other people that their actions are morally wrong, right? Wrong! How can I be so sure that the passage doesn't mean what it seems to mean at first reading? The next few verses, or the context, actually command that followers of Christ determine whether the actions of others are morally right. Verses 3-5 instruct us to get the sin out of our lives so we can help others get the sin out of their lives. Verse 6 warns us to look out for pigs and dogs, which are morally impure people, and verse 20 tells us to inspect the fruit (actions) of others to determine whether they are false or true teachers. Context matters.

In this chapter, we will explore the immediate and larger contexts, and in the next chapter, we will discuss the historical context.

Immediate Context

The immediate context of a passage refers to the verses immediately preceding or following the passage. The size of the immediate context is directly related to the size of the passage you are studying. So, if you are studying two or three verses, it's important to know the topics and main ideas of the two or three verses before the passage, as well as the topics and main ideas of the two or three verses after the passage. If you are studying an entire chapter, it's important to know the topics and ideas of the chapter before and the chapter after. Sometimes, there are no verses before or after the passage you are studying (for example, John 1:1-18), and sometimes, it's obvious there is little or no link between the passages before or after the passage you are studying. For instance, Paul completely changes topics between 2 Corinthians 7 and 8.

Once you've identified which passages should be studied to establish the immediate context of your focus passage, use these questions:
- What's happening or being discussed just before and after the passage I'm studying?
- How does the thought flow from the previous passage, through my passage, to the following passage?
- Has there been a big change in subject from one passage to another?
- How closely related are the subjects and topics in these passages?
- Why might these topics/ideas be located close to one another?

For practice, let's ask these questions of 2 Corinthians 8:9.

> *"For you know the grace of our Lord Jesus Christ, that though he was rich, yet for your sake he became poor, so that you by his poverty might become rich."*

Just before 2 Corinthians 8:9, Paul writes about the sacrificial giving of the churches in Macedonia (verses 1-5) and the opportunity for the church at Corinth to give as well (verses 6-8). Just after verse 9, Paul encourages the Corinthians to finish the act of giving they started earlier (verses 10-12) and he writes that everyone should share what they have with other Christians so that no one will lack anything (13-15). Verse 9 is a bridge between these ideas, because it reminds the reader about the sacrificial giving of Jesus and encourages the reader to follow His example. There hasn't been a change of subject, and the topics are closely related. Verse 9 is there as a reminder of how much has been given to the Corinthian Christians, through Jesus, as they consider their role in giving to the needs of other Christians.

Larger Context
In addition to the immediate context, each passage must be understood in its larger context. This includes the book the passage is located in,

the section of the book, and the entire Bible. So, does that mean that you can't study or understand a single passage until you understand the entire book or section that it's in or even until you understand the entire Bible? Of course not! It just means that we must consider how the larger context influences the passage.

Ask these questions of the passage:
- What is the genre[9] (kind of writing) of the book or section containing this passage?
- Who wrote the book? What other books of the Bible are written by the same author?
- Why was the book written?
- Are there other sections in the Bible that remind you of this book or section?

Again, let's ask these questions of 2 Corinthians 8:9.

2 Corinthians is an epistle, or letter, written by Paul the Apostle, who also wrote many other books in the New Testament. The book was written to address several issues in the church at Corinth. There are other epistles written by Paul, which discuss giving, like Philippians (written to a church in Philippi, Macedonia) and 1 Timothy. First Corinthians, written to the same church, also discusses the offering for the church in Jerusalem.

What if you don't know the answers to any of the questions about the larger context? That's ok, but you should still ask them. Asking questions to which you don't know the answer is part of struggling with the text.

Theological Context: Choosing and Using Systematic Theologies

Part of the larger context is the theological context. At this point, some of you are thinking, "Why is he bringing theology into a perfectly good conversation about studying the Bible?" Many people don't like the word theology, because it sounds too academic. It conjures up images of men in suits and ties sitting at tables in libraries reading books

---

[9]. For a simple but detailed discussion about the different genres in the Bible, see Gordon D. Fee and Douglas Stuart, *How to Read the Bible for All Its Worth*, 3rd edition (Grand Rapids, Mich: Zondervan, 2003).

written by dead people about topics no one can even understand. While those of us in the theological world need to hear that criticism and realize there is some truth to it, we must also recognize that everyone is a theologian; most people are just not intentional about their theology.

Just like meteorology is the study (ology, for logia, meaning "words") of weather (meteor—a Greek word meaning "of the atmosphere"), and biology is the study (ology) of life (bios-a Greek word meaning "life"), theology is simply the study of God (theos is the Greek word for God). Whether we realize it or not, we all have ideas about God, and that means we all have a theology of sorts.

Furthermore, our theology impacts the way we read and interpret biblical passages. For instance, part of my theological identity is Baptist. That means, in part, that I believe only those who have professed faith in Jesus should be baptized, and that when someone is baptized, they should go completely under the water and be brought back up. In other words, I don't believe that baptizing babies is legitimate, because babies can't profess faith in Jesus, and I don't believe that sprinkling a person with water or pouring water over a person's head is a legitimate way of baptizing. So, when I read Matthew 28:18-20, which says,

> *"Go therefore and make disciples of all nations, baptizing them in the name of the Father and of the Son and of the Holy Spirit,"*

I interpret the passage through my Baptist theology to mean that I should only baptize those I am discipling among the nations *after* they profess Jesus as Savior, and that when I baptize them, I should take them completely under the water and bring them back up.

A Presbyterian, however, would interpret the same passage to mean that baptism is a part of the discipleship process that might take place after a person professes faith in Jesus, but it might also take place before a person professes faith in Jesus depending on the situation. A Presbyterian would also see more freedom in the method of baptism, accepting baptism by immersion, sprinkling, or pouring. Who is right? Well, obviously I think Baptists are, or I wouldn't be a Baptist, but honestly, the point of this text is not the timing and method of baptism.

Look at Matthew 28:19 again. It doesn't actually say anything about the timing of baptism relative to a profession of faith, and the only indication of the method of baptism is the word itself (baptism is a transliteration of the Greek word βαπτίζω, which means to immerse under water). In other words, this passage does not really establish either position definitively or deny either position outright. My interpretation of this passage, in part, comes from my theology.

Are we free to just read whatever interpretations we like into the Bible? Of course not. In fact, the only theologies worth considering are those that are developed from intense and extensive study of many different passages, so having a good systematic theology will actually prevent us from developing our own, likely misguided, interpretations. It would be an unwise use of our time to start from scratch and study every passage in the Bible relevant to baptism when Christian scholars have wrestled with this issue for 2,000 years and produced systems of thought, called theologies, which outline all the major passages and issues for us. Neither Baptists nor Presbyterians take their theology about the timing and method of baptism from Matthew 28:19 alone; both systems of theology are based on the study and interpretation of many different passages from the Bible as developed over the last twenty centuries, which makes them both, in one sense, biblically-based and well-developed. The greatest mind in the world could spend a lifetime studying and never reproduce the processes that led to those well-defined positions about baptism, and even if it were possible, there are myriads of other theological issues to be redeveloped.

Thankfully, there's no need to start from scratch and develop your own systematic theology. You just need to evaluate several and choose the system that describes the biblical information in the most accurate and helpful way; and wait, there's more! You don't have to do this all at once. You can, and should, learn and evaluate as you go. Most people start studying the Bible without an intentional, well-developed theology, and it's okay to start there; it's just not a great place to stay. My advice is that as you study the Bible, evaluate different theological systems until you determine which one makes the most sense of the biblical texts.

An Intentional Starting Point

In my opinion, you should start with the theological system of your local church family. If you don't have a local church family, ask God to lead you to one, and start visiting local churches.

Sadly, many people in your local church might not be aware of the theological system of your church, but your pastor should be able to help you. Ask for a basic statement of faith that includes Scripture references, and ask which books you can read to understand more about your church's system of theology, but do that separately from the Inspect the Text step in the Bible study process. As you study the Bible, keep your statement of faith close by, and when you encounter passages dealing with issues addressed in the statement of faith, use the statement as a guide, and look up the passages it references for that particular topic.

Am I saying that one theological system is as good as another so you might as well start with your local church's theological system? No. Absolutely not. If I knew the theological system of your local church, I might strongly encourage you to consider another theological system. However, since I don't know your local church's theological system, and since I'm not bold enough to suggest that my own theological system perfectly accounts for God's revelation in Scripture, I am forced here to point you to a system in which you have already found some type of home. I believe in the power of the Word of God so much, that I believe those of us who study Scripture consistently and submit our preferences and biased beliefs to the authority of the Word of God will arrive at more consensus than disagreement.

Having a well-developed systematic theology is like knowing the rules to a sport. Imagine two people watching the same sporting event—one who knows the rules and one who does not. They both see the same images, but only the one who knows the rules will understand what is going on. Knowing a systematic theology, even a simple one, will help you understand what's going on as you read and study the Bible.

Isn't Theology Just a System Created By Men?

This is a common objection to the study of theology. After all, we want to study the Bible, not what other people have said about the Bible. I could not agree more! This entire book was written to encourage you to actually study the Bible. We, however, have to change this way of thinking when it comes to systems that organize the teachings of the Bible, called systematic theologies or Bible doctrines. They are not the enemies of Bible study—they are a necessary component to successful Bible study.

Let me illustrate. What are north, south, east, and west? The four cardinal directions on earth? What is latitude and longitude? The lines which classify the location of specific points on earth? What are borders? Lines which indicate where the earth is divided between one section and another? The truth is, none of these—the four directions, the latitude and longitude lines, or borders between states and nation—none of these actually exist. They are all imaginary demarcations and systems created by humans to help us navigate our world. Some of them, like the four cardinal directions, have a basis; in fact—in this case, the physical properties of earth's magnetic field, but others, like national borders, are complete fabrications created by humans. What would we do without those manmade systems? We would not be able to fly planes, drive cars, maintain peace and order, or even describe to someone where our home is located.

All theologies[10] are just systems that were created by humans to help us navigate and understand the truths presented in God's Word, but it is hard to imagine what we would do without them. It would be impossible to navigate the complex truths presented in the Bible, and having a conversation with someone else would be virtually impossible since no one would use the same language to describe theological truths. On the other hand, studying theology as an end to itself and not as a guide to the truths of the Bible, would be like exploring the world through a map; and as we all know, even the most accurate maps cannot fully capture the beauty and complexity of the earth. So it is with systems of doctrine and theology. They are helpful guides, but if we want to be explorers and really discover the beauty of the biblical landscape for ourselves, we have to get into the text of the Bible.

Conclusion

---

[10]. By "theologies," I am specifically referring to belief systems, which derive their conclusions from the Bible. My use of this phrase here does not include other religions or even theologies, which claim to be Christian but are not based on the Bible as the sole and final authority.

Imagine meeting the CEO of your dream company, and imagine he offers you your dream job with a fantastic salary and unbelievable benefits. All you need to do is call directly to the unpublished number of his office to set up an interview, and you are in! As a test of your intelligence and determination, though, the CEO lists all the digits in his office phone number in random order. "If you can figure it out, you've got the job" he says as he walks away. No problem, right? Not exactly. There are 3,628,800 different combinations for the 10 digits of a phone number and area code! If you dialed one number every 5 seconds, it would take 210 days to dial all the possible numbers.

Information is important, and so is the order of information. You've done well to follow the order of the process, and it's going to pay off. With each step, your mind becomes more prepared to receive and retain the life-changing truths of God's Word. So far, you've prayed, selected a text to study, read and reread the text, made a list of observations and questions, questioned the text more directly, and considered the literary context. Now there's one more step to inspecting the text—considering the historical context. Keep dialing the numbers, in order, and you will learn to understand the Bible. When the message of the Bible makes sense to you, you will come to love the Bible, and as you come to love the Bible, you will find pleasure and fulfillment in the God of the Bible.

"You make known to me the path of life; in your presence there is fullness of joy; at your right hand are pleasures forevermore." Psalm 16:11

Learn to Love the **BIBLE:**

B-Begin with Prayer and Select a Passage
I- Inspect the Text:
      Read
      List Questions
      Make Observations
      Question the Text
      Consider the Literary Context
B-
L-
E-

Next Steps

1. Read the verses just before and after the passage you've selected.
2. What can you learn about the literary context from those passages?
3. What questions do you still have about the literary context of your selected passage?
4. Pray, asking God for wisdom and understanding of the passage and its literary context.

5

INSPECT THE TEXT PART 4

"54 40 or fight!" Unless you're a US history buff, you probably don't have any idea what that means, but at one time for a particular group of people, that was a rally cry worthy of war, and it helped a relatively unknown politician, James K. Polk, become the 11th president of the United States. Until 1846, the territory that would later become the states of Oregon, Idaho, and Washington was claimed by both the United States and Great Britain. In the 1830's and 40's, thousands of Americans headed west on the Oregon Trail, and the American electorate was ready for a president who would fight for control of the Oregon territory. James K. Polk capitalized on the issue with the pithy phrase, expressing the willingness to go to war unless the British surrendered the territory all the way to the latitude of 54 degrees and 40 seconds. After winning the election, Polk delivered on his promise, sort of, and the United States reached a deal with Great Britain in which the US gained complete control of the territory up to the 49th parallel—350 miles south of the promised 54 degrees and 40 seconds.

The background of "54 40 or fight" illustrates the importance of historical context. That phrase, which was once so important, is now just a historical footnote. Furthermore, without the historical context, it would be nonsensical to anyone outside of the time and culture in which it originated. The same is true of much of the message of the Bible. What might seem like nonsensical words to us come alive with meaning and importance in light of their historical setting.

HISTORICAL CONTEXT

Unlike the immediate and larger context, much of the information about the historical context is located outside of the Bible, and you might not be able to completely understand a text's historical context at this point. This is a great time to remind you, again, that this stage in the process is all about wrestling with the text. So don't get discouraged if you can't answer any of the questions about historical context.

Two Questions About Historical Context

There are two important questions to ask about the historical context: when did the recorded events take place, and when was the passage written? It's not always possible to know the exact answer to these questions, but both internal evidence (evidence inside the book or passage) and external evidence (evidence outside of the book or passage) provide valuable information about the historical setting of much of Scriptures. That leads to the third question raised below, "How can you know?"

When did the events take place?

The most basic question about the historical setting of a passage is, "When did the events take place?" This question does not apply to all passages of the Bible because not all passages record events. For instance, it does not make sense to ask, "When did the events of Proverbs take place?" because there really are no events relayed in the book of Proverbs. It is proper, and very important, to ask "When was the book of Proverbs written?" but that is a separate question we will discuss later.

Most of the Bible, however, is written in a narrative form—it tells stories—and these are stories that actually occurred at real points of time with historical settings. Sometimes, the historical setting is easy to determine to a historically precise degree. The death, burial, and resurrection of Jesus, for instance, certainly took place between 27 and 33 AD. Careful analysis of the text and other sources can narrow the date even more (while surrendering some degree of certainty) to either 30 or 33 AD.

Other times, it is almost impossible to ascribe a date to a particular event like the Tower of Babel recorded in Genesis 11.[11] Even when an event cannot be placed on a calendar, however, the question "when" can be answered in other ways. When did the event occur in relation to other events recorded in the Bible? The Tower of Babel, for instance, was built between the flood and the call of Abram, and that has incredible interpretive importance. Other ways to ask "when" include, in what era of human history did the event occur? Did the events occur under the Law, the Davidic Covenant, the New Covenant, etc.? Sometimes scholars refer to this as an event's place in redemptive history. Which important biblical figures were alive at the time of the event?

Why does that matter?

Knowing when an event occurred, both in actual history and redemptive history, is important interpretive information. Here are four reasons why:

Reason 1

Knowing when an event occurred provides clues for why the event occurred.

Consider the Tower of Babel. Have you ever wondered why God was so upset about people building a tall building? Why did God stop the Tower of Babel and then allow skyscrapers to be built all over the world that are much taller than any tower could have possibly hoped to be in ancient history? Some people read the story and think the people of Babel were trying to build some kind of stairway to Heaven. Mostly, that comes from one missing letter in the KJV of Genesis 11:4 which reads, "And they said, Go to, let us build us a city and a tower, whose top may reach unto heaven."

The word Heaven can mean the place where God lives, and many have mistakenly interpreted it that way in this passage. However, it can also

---

[11]. I am aware of attempts to date the events of Genesis 1-11, but my own study of the Old Testament and dating issues regarding the earliest events recorded in Scripture has led me to the conclusion that there is no clear date given in the Bible for when events like the building of the Tower of Babel occurred.

mean the universe, or simply, the sky. Knowing when the event occurred, in relation to other events, provides evidence that the word should be translated to "heavens" or "sky" as it is in several modern translations. In other words, the people of Babel were trying to build a really tall tower and not a stairway to Heaven. So, how can knowing when the event occurred provide confidence that the third meaning of the word is the correct meaning?

Because the event occurred sometime after the flood, the historical backdrop of that event provides a vital clue. After the flood, God repeated the command for humanity to, "Be fruitful and multiply and fill the earth" Genesis 9:1. God's mandate for humanity was to spread out and fill up the earth. At the Tower of Babel, the sin of the people was not building a tall building, but rather the desire to, "make a name for ourselves, lest we be dispersed over the face of the whole earth" Genesis 11:4b. Furthermore, the result of God's judgment is recorded in Genesis 11:8-10,

"So the Lord dispersed them from there over the face of all the earth, and they left off building the city. Therefore its name was called Babel, because there the Lord confused the language of all the earth. And from there the Lord dispersed them over the face of all the earth."

The people of Babel were in direct, corporate disobedience against God's command to multiply and fill the earth. God said go, and they said no! Knowing that this event took place closely after the flood provides the clue we need to properly understand the sin of the people at Babel. It's not always wrong to build a tall tower, but it's always wrong to disobey a command of God.

Reason 2

Knowing when an event occurred provides depth to the account of the event.

David, Israel's great king, committed adultery with Bathsheba and murdered her husband, Uriah, as a part of the cover up. God sent Nathan the prophet to confront David over his sin, which led to David's repentance. In Samuel's account of this event (2 Samuel 11-12), only a few verses separate David's sin from Nathan's confrontation so a casual reading of the text might lead the reader to think Nathan confronted David right away.

That's how I imagined the story for many years: David sinned, Nathan confronted David, and David repented and started the restoration process. Then, someone showed me that several months, perhaps even a year, passed between David's sin and Nathan's confrontation. By the time Nathan confronted David, the baby had already been born (2 Samuel 12:15), so at least 9 months had passed from David's initial act of adultery to Nathan's confrontation.

David's sin teaches an invaluable lesson, and understanding that months passed between sin and confession adds great depth to the account of the story.

- David, who loved God and God's presence so much, lived with a cold, sin-stricken heart, which kept him away from the presence of God for a long time.
- God allowed months to pass in which David felt no godly sorrow over his sin.
- For a short time, God allowed David to look like a hero who came to Bathsheba's rescue after her husband was killed in battle. To most people in the kingdom, it looked like David had adopted Uriah's son, thereby granting him all the rights and privileges of being raised in the king's palace.
- David's words of repentance recorded in Psalm 51 become even more powerful upon the realization that those words only came after months of cold-heartedness.
- David's description in Psalm 32:3-4 gains emphasis and depth when the reader thinks of months passing without repentance.

When did Nathan confront David about his sin? While no one can point to a date on the calendar, knowing it took place 9 months or more after David's sin adds depth and understanding to the story.

Reason 3

Knowing when an event occurred provides tools for understanding other passages and events.

The book of Ruth opens with a line that most modern readers ignore: "In the days when the judges ruled" (Ruth 1:1). The story of Ruth's marriage to Boaz and Naomi's redemption through their marriage is one of the most beautiful stories in all of literature. It's not intended, however, to be just a beautiful love story with a happy ending. One of the major themes of the book of Ruth is God's work in the darkest times.

The days of the judges were some of the darkest days in Israel's history, and students of the book of Judges are often left wondering if anything good can come from a time when *"everyone did what was right in his own eyes"* because there was no king (Judges 21:25). Knowing when the story of Ruth occurred, however, reveals that underneath all the chaos of the time of the judges, God was working to bring a king to Israel. The first child born to Boaz and Ruth was named Obed, and the closing verses of Ruth explain, *"Boaz fathered Obed, Obed fathered Jesse, and Jesse fathered David"* (Ruth 4:21-22). Boaz was the great grandfather of King David, and even more importantly, Boaz was the ancestor of the King of Kings, Jesus.

Reason 4

Knowing when an event occurred affects the theological interpretation of a passage.

Have you ever wondered why modern Christians don't witness God's work through supernatural means as much as the early church or God's people in the Old Testament? I sure have. I would read the stories from the Bible about miracles and other supernatural events and think something was wrong with me or something was wrong with my church. As I started taking a closer look at Scripture, I recognized a faulty assumption in my thinking. I assumed, as many Christians do, supernatural events occurred in the Old Testament and the early church consistently, year after year, week after week, and even day after day.

So how often did God work through supernatural means in the lives of His people in Scripture? When you take a closer look at the timeline of events, it wasn't as often or as consistent as it first seems. For instance, the book of Acts seems like the account of one miraculous event after another, and it is—especially the early chapters. What may not be apparent, however, at the first reading, is that the book of Acts covers a 30-year period! Between the stories of the supernatural are many untold stories of faithful Christians following Jesus without experiencing any miraculous events other than their salvation and union with Christ (which is without a doubt the greatest miracle anyone can experience).

What about the Old Testament? There are many, many miracles and supernatural events in the Old Testament, but they cover thousands of years! A careful look at the timeline of Scripture and miracles reveals four periods of time when miracles seemed to happen all the time—the time around the Exodus, the time of Elijah and Elisha, the ministry of Jesus, and the birth of the church. Other than those periods, miracles were either not recorded or were very rare.

Consider the life and ministry of Nehemiah. God worked through natural means (relationships, politics, good administrative skills, wisdom, leadership, etc.) to rebuild the walls of Jerusalem. God could have miraculously rebuilt the walls just as He miraculously destroyed the walls of Jericho centuries earlier, but He chose to work through His people to accomplish His plan. Nehemiah was faithfully following God; God was using Nehemiah for His purposes; the task was seemingly impossible, but God chose not to intervene supernaturally.

But what about the New Testament? Once the Holy Spirit came in Acts 2, miracles were a common occurrence, right? Yes, for a while. As the story of the early church unfolds in the book of Acts, the consistency with which miracles occur decreases steadily. Well, what about Jesus? He was always working miracles, so doesn't that mean whenever Jesus is around, miracles will happen? The ministry of Jesus included miracles on a more consistent basis than any other period of Scripture, but Jesus lived for 30 years before performing His first miracle. During that time, Jesus was faithful to God's laws, He prayed and meditated on Scripture, and He was God, with all the power of God, but Jesus did not perform any miracles in those first 30 years.

Knowing when events occurred shapes theology by providing a more complete picture of God's work and His word. Studying the timing and consistency of supernatural, miraculous work in the Bible reveals that God can do anything He wants at anytime He wants to do it, but He chooses, for His purposes, to do more miraculous work at particular times than at other times.

Observing the timing of miracles, teaches us to see God's work through natural means, as no less His work. After Nehemiah led the people to complete the wall, the Bible says, "So the wall was finished . . . in fifty-two days. And when all our enemies heard of it . . . they perceived that this work had been accomplished with the help of our God" Nehemiah 6:15-16. The people built the wall without angels, without miracles, and without a thundering voice from heaven commanding them, but it was apparent to the nations around them that God was involved.

How can you know?

It is important to know when the events of the Bible occurred, but how can you know? Wouldn't it be nice if the books of the Bible had time stamps on them? It might be surprising to discover that many of the books do, but we often don't recognize them or know how to read them.

Old Testament

The Old Testament is divided into the Books of Moses (Genesis-Deuteronomy), the Historical Books (Joshua-Esther), Wisdom Literature (Job-Song of Songs), the Major Prophets (Isaiah-Daniel), and the Minor Prophets (Hosea-Malachi). Each section deals with dates and historical setting differently.

The Books of Moses-context clues

The most difficult events in the entire Bible to date are those found in the Books of Moses. When was the world created? When was the flood? When did God scatter the people out of Babel? When did Terah, Abram's father, leave Ur? When was Joseph in Egypt? When did the Exodus and conquest occur?

Although it's impossible to be certain about the timing of these events, context clues provide a range of possible dates for many of the events. For instance, consider the dating of the Exodus. Using context clues, most scholars believe the Exodus occurred in either the 15th century B.C. or the 13th century B.C., so there is a range of about 200 years during which the Exodus most likely occurred.

More importantly, clues within the stories date the events in relation to each other. Regardless of when the Exodus occurred, Moses was born around 80 years before the Exodus and died after the Exodus, just before the conquest of Canaan. Joseph lived in Egypt about 400 years earlier, and the events in the book of Judges took place just after the conquest of Canaan.

How Was I Supposed to Know All of That?

Some of you reading this grew up hearing sermons and going to Sunday School, and you probably knew about the dates of the Exodus, Moses' life, Joseph's life, etc. Others might be thinking, "It's good that you know that, but I never went to Sunday School or seminary!" I suppose even those of you who understand the basics about Joseph, Moses, the Exodus, and Joshua would like to know how you are supposed to unravel complex clues across several books to determine the historical setting of less familiar passages; and you are right—it would take years for any one person to string together all the obvious context clues in just one book of the Bible. Don't give up. Hang in there. Help is on the way. Remember that in this section, we are learning to struggle with the text. It doesn't matter if you can't find the answers at this point in the process. What matters is that you understand the importance of asking the questions. Remember, "Wax on. Wax off."

The Historical Books

Thankfully, the authors of the Historical Books often state the dates of the events they record. For instance, the book of Ruth begins with, *"In the days when the judges ruled"* Ruth 1:1. Other books give even more specific dates such as Ezra, which begins, *"In the first year of Cyrus king of Persia"* Ezra 1:1. Although the life and reign of Cyrus is well known to history, and "the first year of Cyrus" almost certainly refers to the year he conquered Babylon, 539 B.C., at this point in the process, it's not so important that you know the specific date, but it would be wise to make a note of the historical reference.

Wisdom Literature

Like the Books of Moses, the Wisdom Literature books of the Old
Testament do not state the year in which the events they record
occurred, so dating relies on context clues.

The Prophets

Some of the most overlooked verses in the Bible are the opening verses
of the Old Testament prophetic books. The book of Isaiah begins,
*"The vision of Isaiah the son of Amoz, which he saw concerning Judah and
Jerusalem in the days of Uzziah, Jotham, Ahaz, and Hezekiah, kings of Judah"*
Isaiah 1:1. These verses describe, with great precision, when the
prophecies recorded in the books that follow were received. The verses
are overlooked because the names of the kings mentioned are strange
and meaningless to most modern readers. However, these verses are
ancient time stamps, which provide the date and situation in which the
prophets did their work.

Major Prophets

All of the books of the Major Prophets, except Lamentations, state the
date of the events they cover in the opening verses. Ezekiel even
provides the month and day he began receiving the message God gave
him. The Major Prophets, however, cover so much time and so many
events, that it is helpful to look for other dates throughout the books.
In other words, it's best to take a section-by-section or even a chapter-
by-chapter approach to determine when the events recorded occurred.

In Jeremiah, for instance, the chapters are not arranged chronologically,
and the events of one chapter often occur before the events of the
preceding chapter. Jeremiah 24 records events and prophecies that
occurred after Nebuchadnezzar of Babylon had taken a man named
Jeconiah, who was serving as king of Israel, to Babylon as a prisoner.
The events of chapter 25, the very next chapter, however, took place in
"the first year of Nebuchadnezzar king of Babylon" when Jehoiakim,
Jeconiah's father, was still the king of Israel (Jeremiah 25:1).

Minor Prophets

Like the Major Prophets, six of the Minor Prophets state the date of
the events. Hosea, Amos, Micah, Zephaniah, Haggai, and Zechariah all
give the names of rulers under which they prophesied. Most of the
other Minor Prophets provide significant context clues to the date of
the events they describe. The most notable exception is Joel, who
describes a locust invasion that could have occurred at just about any
time in Israel's history.

New Testament

Unlike the Old Testament, only a few New Testament books state the
time in which the events occurred.

The Gospel of Luke and Acts

No New Testament author is more detailed about dates than Luke,
who wrote the Gospel of Luke and the book of Acts. He often includes
historical dating references like Luke 2:1-2, *"In those days a decree went out
from Caesar Augustus that all the world should be registered. This was the first
registration when Quirinius was governor of Syria."* Luke also records the
number of days between and during events, making it easier to
understand the chronology of the early church.

The Other Gospels

Matthew, Mark, and John are given their historical setting from context
clues and close comparison with Luke and one another.

Paul's Epistles

Occasionally, as in Galatians 1 and 2, Paul describes historical events
that occurred in his lifetime, so it is appropriate to ask, "When did this
event happen?" In those cases, passages can be compared with other
New Testament passages (especially Acts) to determine when the
events occurred relative to other New Testament events.

Other Epistles

There are only a handful of events mentioned in the other epistles, and
there are no time markers given for those events. Determining when

the events took place is a subjective process of cross comparing other texts and historical data to look for matching historical situations.

And Then There's Revelation!

Given the complexity of Revelation's timeline (things that are, things that are to take place after this) and the vast overemphasis on times and dates, I encourage you to learn what Jesus meant when He said,

> *"It is not for you to know times or seasons that the Father has fixed by his own authority. But you will receive power when the Holy Spirit has come upon you, and you will be my witnesses in Jerusalem and in all Judea and Samaria, and to the end of the earth."* Acts 1:7-8

While it can be helpful to study the historical setting of John's exile to Patmos mentioned in 1:9, or the information about the cities of the seven churches in chapters 2 and 3, we must resist being dogmatic about future, past, and especially present fulfillments of prophecies given in Revelation. The best way to learn the background details about John and the churches mentioned in Revelation is long-term study of the New Testament. In other words, if you study other books first, you will come to Revelation armed with background knowledge that will help you understand the book better.

When was the book written?

At first, it might seem like we just answered that question because we invested several pages discussing when the events of the Bible occurred. However, this is a closely related, yet different question, "When was the book written?"

Think about modern books. One of my favorite books is "Lincoln on Leadership" by Donald T. Phillips, which is obviously about the 16th president of the United States, Abraham Lincoln. Many books have been written about Lincoln, and most of them, like "Lincoln on Leadership" published in 1992, were written long after his death. Phillips, the author of this particular book about Lincoln, applied stories from Lincoln's life and time in the White House to leadership challenges of the 1990's. In the same way, events that occurred throughout the history of God's people were often revisited in the biblical writings years or even centuries later to teach eternal truths to the contemporary people of God.

Why does that matter?

Knowing when a book was written is different from knowing when the events occurred. Both are important, but knowing when a book was written gives us more of an idea about the purpose of the book than just knowing when the events occurred.

Think about the book of Genesis—specifically Genesis chapter 3, which is one of the most important chapters in the Bible. Moses wrote it sometime after the Exodus and before his death, which was just before the people of Israel entered the Promised Land. The chapter, which deals with the fall of humanity into sin, resonates throughout the rest of the Bible and all of human history, but why did God wait until that particular point in history to reveal the events of humanity's fall into sin? Like Adam and Eve, the Jewish people were preparing to enter a land God had given them and live under a covenant. The story of Adam and Eve was a tool God used to remind them that under a covenant of works, like the Law, obedience produces blessing and fellowship with God while disobedience results in God's curse and expulsion from the land.

How can you know?

Learning when books of the Bible were written can be even more difficult than determining when the events occurred, but the approach is similar.

Sometimes it is stated

Some books, like the books of Moses, provide enough details to determine their date of writing. Moses wrote the first five books of the Bible, and most of the material did not exist until after the Exodus and gathering at Mount Sinai, so it's obvious the books were written after the Exodus and before the death of Moses.[12] The calendar date of the

---

[12]. Some sections of the Books of Moses were added or edited after Moses' death (such as the record of Moses' death and the mourning of the nation after his death), but the majority of the material was completed in his lifetime.

Books of Moses is not as easy to determine, but knowing the date relative to other events is, and that is more important for interpretive purposes.

Sometimes context clues are clear

If a book does not clearly state its date of writing, sometimes context clues provide an almost certain date. For instance, 2 Timothy is not dated, but Paul speaks so clearly about his near and certain death in the letter that it was obviously written just before Paul's death. Paul died in the mid 60's AD, so the book was written around the same time.

Sometimes experts are best

If the book does not state the date of writing and the context clues are not clear at all, the experts are probably the best source. For instance, the book of James was most likely written by the half-brother of Jesus who died in 62 AD, but scholars have many theories about when the book was written. In such cases, it is best to consult the experts, learn the different opinions, and move on realizing God did not reveal the specific date or circumstance of writing with certainty, and that's okay! God has His reasons. Perhaps some books, like James, have such a universal and timeless application that the Lord did not want readers to be tempted to disregard clear teachings as only applying to other people in other times and other situations. So, use the commentaries and scholars to help you determine when some books were written, but not yet! "Wax on. Wax off!"

Conclusion

"It takes more than that to kill a bull moose!" Why would Teddy Roosevelt, one of our nation's most beloved presidents, say something so strange? What is the amazing story behind this statement, and how did his actions at that time reshape American politics? Go ahead, a simple Internet search should give you all the pertinent facts surrounding the quote. Historical context matters, and taking time to ask when the events occurred and when the book was written will help you understand and come to love the timeless truth of the Bible and the God revealed in the Bible. In the next chapter, we will take one more step to Inspect the Text by exploring the authorship, recipients and occasion of biblical passages.

Learn to Love the **BIBLE**:

B-Begin with Prayer and Select a Passage
I- Inspect the Text:
       Read
       List Questions
       Make Observations
       Question the Text
       Consider the Literary Context
       Consider the Historical Context
B-
L-
E-

Next Steps

The book of Genesis was written as the Jewish people prepared to enter the Promised Land. Using that information, read Genesis 15:12-12-16 and reflect on the following questions, praying for wisdom and insight as you study:

1. Abram was sleeping in the Promised Land when God spoke to him. Why would this passage be important to the Jewish people preparing to enter the Promised Land?
2. How would knowing God's words to Abram in verse 13-14 bring comfort to the Jewish people who had recently suffered as slaves in Egypt?
3. The Amorites were people living in the Promised Land (Canaan) in the time of Abram. They were still there when the Jewish people entered the land, and God commanded the Jewish people to destroy them. What does verse 16 teach about the wickedness of the people in Canaan and the righteousness of God?
4. If you were a Jewish person commanded to destroy the Amorites, how would verse 16 help you understand God's justice?

6

INSPECT THE TEXT PART 5

FOUND magazine, which collects and publishes misplaced notes, began on a snowy Chicago night in the year 2000 when Davy Rothbart found a note on his car's windshield after work. The note was addressed to someone named Mario, who obviously drove a car similar to Davy's car, and it was from a girl named Amber, who was apparently Mario's girlfriend. In the note, which is too intense to share here, Amber expressed her shock and anger at seeing Mario's car parked at "her place." After all, Amber reminds Mario, "You said you have to work." Oops. Poor Mario.[13]

Amber made one small, but crucial mistake which led her to an even larger mistake—she misidentified the audience and situation of her intended communication. The biblical authors wrote with particular audiences and situations in mind, and knowing the author, recipients, and occasion of a message, is vitally important to determining the meaning of the message.

AUTHORSHIP, RECIPIENTS, AND OCCASION

This chapter is the last section of the Inspect the Text discussion, and obviously by this point, the text has been thoroughly inspected! As we discuss authorship, recipients, and occasion, you'll notice overlap with

---

[13]. http://foundmagazine.com/who-we-are/

subjects covered in previous chapters, but even if you've already asked and begun to answer these questions, this chapter will give you tools to find even more answers.

Authorship

The Bible is not a book. It is a collection of books written by approximately 40 different authors who spoke at least 3 different languages and wrote from Europe, Africa, and Asia over a 1,400 year period. Some authors, like Solomon and Paul, wrote multiple books, and some authors, like Heman (that's right, I said Heman) only wrote one chapter.

Why does it matter?

This may seem obvious, but knowing who wrote a particular book or section of the Bible can be a very helpful interpretive tool. Whenever I look for a modern book, I want to know who wrote the book before investing time reading it. A few years ago, I pre-ordered a book without even looking closely at the title, just because it was written by two people I respect, and it was one of the best books I've read on church strategy.

The authors of books in the Bible were musicians, kings, fishermen turned disciples, apostles, priests, prophets, and shepherds. They were rich, poor, and working class. Some were poets while others were only able to write in simple sentences. God chose these authors for a reason, and it's important to know about them as we read and study what they wrote. Knowing about the author of a book or section of the Bible provides clues about the author's intent, state of mind, focus, and style, among other attributes. All of these contribute to meaning and interpretation.

How can you know?

The only way to know for certain who wrote a particular book or section in the Bible is if the book or section identifies its author. Thankfully, this is true of many of the books.

Paul, for instance, opened his letters with a greeting which included his name.

"Paul, a servant of Christ Jesus, called to be an apostle, set apart for the gospel of God." Romans 1:1

Similar statements can be found in the first verses of all of his letters, and most of the books which identify their authors do so in the opening verses. The Books of Moses are the exception because they identify Moses and the author in several places scattered throughout the books, but only mention Moses' authorship at the beginning of a book once— the book of Deuteronomy.

Which James?

Sometimes a book or section identifies its author but does not provide enough detail to identify the person with certainty. That is the case with James 1:1, which reads, "James, a servant of God and of the Lord Jesus Christ." There are at least 4 different James' mentioned in the New Testament who are followers of Jesus, and there is no doubt that many other men named James who followed Jesus but were not mentioned in the Bible. So, of all the possible James, which one wrote the book bearing that name?

Scholars use textual clues, church history, and a process of elimination to make good guesses, but they often disagree. It is best to consult the experts (remember the process!) and choose an opinion. For what it's worth, I feel certain that James the half-brother of Jesus wrote the book of James.

What About Anonymous Books?

Many books in the Bible are anonymous. This includes most of the Historical Books in the Old Testament *and* all four Gospels in the New Testament. That's right— go ahead and take a look in Matthew, Mark, Luke, and John. The authors did not sign their names anywhere! Remember, the titles in our Bibles were added, along with the chapters and verses, as tools to help us.

So, did your Sunday School teacher, pastor, or AWANA leader mislead you? Well, not really. (If you didn't grow up in church, just ignore the reference to AWANA). More than likely, the four Gospels were written by Matthew, Mark, Luke, and John. There is a reason early Christians felt confident enough to put those names as titles. Context clues and church history identify these men as the likely authors.

Consider the Gospel of John. It is true that John the Apostle, the brother of James (don't confuse him with John the Baptist who is mentioned in the first chapter) is never mentioned as the author. In fact, he is never mentioned by name at all in the Gospel of John! Each time John the Apostle is part of the story, his name is excluded. John is called "the other disciple," and "the disciple whom Jesus loved," but he is never mentioned by name. Then, in John 21:24, the book identifies the disciple whom Jesus loved as the author of the book. It seems John intended for us to do some homework in order to determine the author.

Like the Gospels, other anonymous books must be analyzed using the best available historical data and context clues to determine the likely author.

Now What?

Once an author is identified, it's important to learn about the author. What is his background? What other books did he write? Why did God choose him to write this book or section of the Bible? Learning about the human tool God used to write His Word will help you understand God's message through the Bible. Leave the commentaries and study Bibles aside for now, and use a concordance or an online searchable Bible like blueletterbible.org to search for passages where the author is mentioned.

The Situation and Recipients

The question of why the book was written (situation) is so closely related to the question of to whom the book was written (recipients), that it's best to consider them together.

The situation is sometimes called the occasion or sitz im leben, which is a German phrase meaning, "the setting in life." The situation often arises from what the recipients of the book are experiencing, and sometimes the situation is about the issue or issues that caused the author to write the book or letter.

Why does it matter?

Moses, David, Jeremiah, John, Paul, Peter, and the other authors of
Scripture wrote in response to real life situations facing real people.
When we pick up the Bible to read or study, we are naturally more
concerned with our own lives, and we tend to impose our situations on
the text as we study and make ourselves the target audience of the
passage. For example, when we read Philippians 4:13, *"I can do all things
through him who strengthens me,"* we naturally think of all the challenges we
are facing—the big test, a sporting event, financial issues, etc.—and we
treat this verse like a Rocky quote.

> "Going that one more round when you don't think you can -
> that's what makes all the difference in your life." Rock Balboa,
> preparing to fight the 6'5" Russian fighting machine, Ivan
> Drago in Rocky IV

No matter what, I can do this! I can ace the test, I can win the game,
and I can knock out my student loan debt or a 6'5" 260lb Russian
fighting machine. I can do all things through Jesus!

If you've thought of Philippians 4:13 in this way, you've done so partly
because you've not considered the situation of the letter or its original
recipients. Paul, while in prison, wrote to thank the church at Philippi
for their financial support of his ministry and to let them know how
much it was helping him. In this case, since many of us are very familiar
with Philippians 4:13, the Message paraphrase will help us see the
passage from a different perspective. While I don't recommend
paraphrases such as the Message for regular reading and study, they can
be helpful compliments to a good, reliable translation. Read verses 10-
14 in the Message:

> *"I'm glad in God, far happier than you would ever guess—happy that
> you're again showing such strong concern for me. Not that you ever quit
> praying and thinking about me. You just had no chance to show it.
> Actually, I don't have a sense of needing anything personally. I've learned
> by now to be quite content whatever my circumstances. I'm just as happy
> with little as with much, with much as with little. I've found the recipe for
> being happy whether full or hungry, hands full or hands empty. Whatever
> I have, wherever I am, I can make it through anything in the One who
> makes me who I am. I don't mean that your help didn't mean a lot to*

me—it did. It was a beautiful thing that you came alongside me in my troubles."

As we understand the situation behind the letter, it becomes apparent that the message of Philippians 4:13 is not that we will always come out on top, win the game, get the girl, beat the disease, get the job, pass the test, etc. The meaning is that, through the strength of Jesus, Paul endured many difficult situations, including intense suffering such as imprisonment. Furthermore, we realize that verse 13 is not the main point of the book, chapter, or even the paragraph. It is a supporting idea to the main idea: Paul is thankful for their financial support.

Every passage has one meaning and multiple implications and applications, and it's in these, where passages intersect our lives. We aren't Apostles suffering in a 1st century Roman prison, and we aren't a 1st century church in a Roman city, so the meaning of the passage doesn't immediately intersect our lives. However, we do suffer, and we are called to contribute to the work of the kingdom as it advances, so the implications and applications of this passage apply to our lives. Chapter 8 discusses the process for drawing these out in more detail.

At first, it seems as though we've taken one of the most exciting passages in Scripture and made it really boring. Think about it. In just a few short paragraphs, we've gone from quoting Rocky and fighting Ivan Drago to giving money to missionaries. The truth is, however, we've taken the focus off ourselves and our problems and focused our attention on God's kingdom purpose of reaching the nations with the gospel. Not only is that the opposite of boring, it also frees us from our narcissistic hijacking of God's Word for building our own kingdom and accomplishing our own purposes. The situation behind the passage, and the original audience of the passage both impact meaning significantly.

How can you know?

Determining the intended recipients and situation of a book is like determining the author; sometimes the recipients and purpose are stated; sometimes they are clearly implied from context clues, sometimes it's difficult to know without the help of scholars, and sometimes it's impossible to know for certain.

Consider three examples. All of Paul's letters state a recipient and most even state the situation either directly or indirectly. 1 Corinthians 1:2 identifies the recipients of that letter as *"the church of God that is in Corinth."* The occasion or situation of Paul's writing to the church at Corinth is revealed in 1:10-12, where Paul explains that he wrote in response to reports of division, and 7:1, where Paul indicates that he was responding to questions that he received from the church in a letter.

Jeremiah, on the other hand, is written with a clear audience and into a specific situation, but those are not directly stated. Even a casual reading of Jeremiah, however, reveals that his prophecies and the book containing them were written to Jewish people before and just after the Babylonian Exile. As the book progresses, it's easy to guess that Jeremiah's purpose in recording these prophecies in written form is to give hope to those in Exile, because Jeremiah was right about Judah's Exile, and he will prove to be right about Judah's return to the land and restoration.

The book of James is an altogether different issue. Virtually nothing in the book itself gives any clear reference to the people or situation to which the book was written. There are subtle clues, but they are the type of clues that only experienced scholars are likely to recognize. Does that mean that you should just run to a commentary or study Bible? No. Not first. Stick with the process; look for clues and get an idea of the type of people and characteristics of the situation being addressed. A close reading of James will indicate that the recipients include the wealthy and the poor, people who know the Old Testament stories, and teachers. Readers, without the help of scholars, will also be able to determine at least part of the situation—the recipients have misunderstood the relationship between faith and works, and there is tension between the rich and poor in the church.

Conclusion

Have you ever been at the airport and overhead a stranger's phone conversation? Of course not! That would be eavesdropping and would be completely rude! But just imagine that in a moment of weakness and boredom while waiting for your flight to leave, you happened to overhear just a few moments of a phone conversation. While you might be able to determine something about the meaning of what's being said, it's difficult, if not impossible, to really get the true meaning of what's being said, because you don't know anything about the people talking, and you are only hearing one side of the conversation. Reading the Bible can be just like that. The more we learn about the person who wrote the book and the people, places, and situations on the other side of the conversation, the more we will understand what's being said. Understanding the authorship, recipients, and situation of the passages you study will open up your understanding of the Bible in a completely new way.

What we've done so far is to deconstruct, or take apart the text, to look at it from many different angles. It's like we've opened the box to a 10,000 piece puzzle, spread all the pieces out on the table, and started to examine them. Now, it's time to start the process of putting the puzzle together. In the next chapter, we will take the first step in that process—Build an Outline.

Learn to Love the **BIBLE**:

B-Begin with Prayer and Select a Passage
I- Inspect the Text:
    Read
    List Questions
    Make Observations
    Question the Text
    Consider the Literary Context
    Consider the Historical Context
    Explore the Authorship, Recipients, and Situation
B-
L-
E-

Next Steps

Using only a Bible with no other tools, answer the following questions:

1. Who was the author of Galatians?
2. Who was the author of Ecclesiastes?
3. Find a Psalm that has a stated author.
4. Who was the author of Proverbs 31?

5. Do the first few verses of 1 Samuel identify the author?
6. Scan the book of James looking for references to wealth and poverty, faith and works, and the Old Testament. What do these references tell us about the recipients and situation?

7

BUILD AN OUTLINE

"For every minute spent organizing, an hour is earned."
Benjamin Franklin

"The oldest building in the western hemisphere is right here in North Miami, Florida." The first time I heard someone make that bold declaration, I knew it couldn't be true—but it is. The ancient Spanish Monastery, completed in 1141 AD is located less than five miles from my home. That's in the United States—in Florida—in Miami! Of all the large influential cities in the world, Miami is one of the youngest, and it certainly wasn't around in 1141 AD. So, what's the story? In 1925, William Randolph Hearst purchased the monastery, which was located in northern Spain, took it apart block by block, packed it into 11,000 crates, and shipped it to the United States. After sitting in storage for a few years, eventually the building was reconstructed in its present location.

Can you imagine the immense task of reconstructing an entire monastery, which includes several buildings, from blocks packed in 11,000 crates? The project was so monumental that a 1953 issue of Time Magazine called it "the biggest jigsaw puzzle in history." Thankfully, the builders had some help. As the monastery was taken apart, each crate was numbered to correspond to its location in the monastery. Although the task was not easy, having numbered crates gave the builders an idea of how to organize the material.[14] That's what an outline does; it gives us a tangible way to approach the otherwise daunting task of understanding a biblical passage.

BUILD AN OUTLINE

The purpose of an outline is twofold—first, it organizes ideas and thoughts, and second, it makes those ideas and thoughts more manageable and accessible. Consider a shopping list: one dozen eggs, two pairs of jeans, one extension cord, one pound of flour, two bags of chips, one brown belt, fifty 2" wood screws, two 8" 2x4s, one loaf of bread, one saw blade, one pair of dress shoes, and one jar of peanut butter. If you head out for a morning of errands with those items randomly scribbled on a scrap piece of paper, or even worse, "memorized," you're likely to be very inefficient if not ineffective in your tasks.

Consider the same list organized into a simple outline:

1. Items from the clothing store
   a. Two pairs of jeans
   b. One brown belt
   c. One pair of dress shoes
2. Items from the hardware store
   a. One extension cord
   b. Fifty 2" wood screws
   c. Two 8" 2x4s
   d. One saw blade
3. Items from the grocery store
   a. One dozen eggs
   b. One pound of flour
   c. Two bags of chips
   d. One loaf of bread
   e. One jar of peanut butter

Now, your errands are clearer, and did you notice you need to pick up three things at the first store, four things at the second store, and five things at your last stop? That makes it more manageable and even more

---

[14]. http://www.spanishmonastery.com/history

memorable. Outlining biblical passages will make them more accessible, manageable, and memorable.

You Don't Have to Be an English Whiz

Most people are intimidated by the idea of building an outline. I've often stared at a passage for what seems like hours wondering if there's any way I can create an outline. How does all this information fit together? How is it organized? What is the author's thought process? As you wrestle with these questions, it's important to remember that you're not trying to create the organizational structure—you're just looking for what's already there. Unlike the shopping list example above, the authors have already organized the information for us. We are just trying to recognize the organization that is already there. Also, if we work to create an outline and it misses the entire point of the passage and makes a train wreck out of the author's thought process, that's ok. It's more important to wrestle with the structure than it is to get everything just right. That's what the next step, Learn from the Experts, is designed to accomplish. As you compare your outline to those of other Bible students, you'll be evaluating and refining your own outline, and you'll recognize any glaring errors in your own thought process.

Step One: Break Down the Passage

The first step to outlining a passage is to copy and paste the passage into a word processor document. Then, you can break it down by its linguistic structure. Wait, don't panic—yes, I just said "linguistic structure," but it's not as bad as it sounds. For some of you, that may sound more like Italian food than something related to Bible study. "I'll have the linguistic structure, and can I get a salad with that?" The phrase just refers to the way the word and sentences are organized, and thankfully, breaking down the linguistic structure is easier done than said.

Depending on the length of the passage and your level of language arts skills, you can take several approaches. The simplest approach is to break the passage at its punctuation marks. For example, Ephesians 1:20-21 reads,

"That he worked in Christ when he raised him from the dead and seated him at his right hand in the heavenly places, far above all rule and authority and power and dominion, and above every name that is named, not only in this age but also in the one to come."

There are three punctuation marks (three commas) in those two verses, and below, the passage has been separated at those commas. The only real decision that has to be made is whether the idea after the comma is a new idea of equal importance to the idea before or if it is an idea that supplements the previous main idea in some way. I've tabbed the supplemental ideas over so they are situated under the ideas they support.

Ephesians 1:20-21 Broken at Punctuation Marks
That he worked in Christ when he raised him from the dead and seated him at his right hand in the heavenly places,
> *far above all rule and authority and power and dominion,*
> *and above every name that is named,*
>> *not only in this age but also in the one to come.*

Notice that with the small, easy task of breaking the passage at the punctuation marks, the message and meaning of the passage becomes clearer—Jesus' place in heaven is above all rulers, and all names, not only names in this age, but also names in eternity.

With just a little more work, you can break the passage at the punctuation marks and the conjunctions, and get even more insight into the passage.

Ephesians 1:20-21 Broken at Punctuation Marks and Conjunctions
That he worked in Christ when he raised him from the dead and seated him at his right hand in the heavenly places,
> *far above all rule*
> *and authority*
> *and power*
> *and dominion,*
> *and above every name that is named,*
>> *not only in this age*
>> *but also in the one to come.*

By simply breaking the passage at the punctuation marks and conjunctions, we've organized the verses in a way that reveals the two main points of the passage, situated farthest to the left (Jesus was raised from the dead, and Jesus was seated in Heaven) and several sub-points.

There are two additional steps you can take, depending on your proficiency in languages arts and the length of the passage. These steps will add more clarity, but they aren't necessary to grasp the main ideas of the passage.

First, you can break the passage at prepositional phrases and similar phrases. This is more art than science, because it depends on each reader's approach to the passage. Again, consider Ephesians 1:20-21.

Ephesians 1:20-21 Broken at Punctuation Marks, Conjunctions, & Phrases

That he worked
> *in Christ*
> *when he*
>> *raised him*
>>> *from the dead*
>> *and seated him*
>>> *at his right hand*
>>> *in the heavenly places,*
>>> *far above*
>>>> *all rule*
>>>> *and authority*
>>>> *and power*
>>>> *and dominion,*
>>>> *and above every name*
>>>>> *that is named,*
>>>>>> *not only*
>>>>>>> *in this age*
>>>>>> *but also*
>>>>>>> *in the one*
>>>>>>>> *to come.*

This strategy revealed one key truth not as evident from the other steps—these verses are not just about what Jesus accomplished, but they are about something God accomplished through Jesus (*That he worked*).

Use table 5 to determine which strategy to use when breaking down a text. Match the number of verses in the passage you are studying with the left-hand column and your level of language arts proficiency with the numbers in the top row.

Table 5: Suggested Levels of Breaking Down a Passage

# of Verses	Level of Language Arts Proficiency (1-Beginner, 5-Expert)				
	1	2	3	4	5
1-5	Break the Passage at the Punctuation Marks	Break the Passage at the Punctuation Marks	Break Passage at Punctuation Marks, Conjunctions, Prepositional Phrases, and Other Phrases.	Break Passage at Punctuation Marks, Prepositional Phrases, & Other Phrases, Diagram Sentences that Seem Significant or Difficult	Diagram the Sentences
6-15	Choose a Shorter Passage	Break the Passage at the Punctuation Marks	Break the Passage at the Punctuation Marks	Break the Passage at the Punctuation Marks, Conjunctions, Prepositional Phrases, and Other Phrases.	Break Passage at Punctuation Marks, Prepositional Phrases, & Other Phrases, Diagram Sentences that Seem Significant or Difficult
16-30	Choose a Shorter Passage	Choose a Shorter Passage	Break the Passage at the Punctuation Marks	Break the Passage at the Punctuation Marks	Break Passage at Punctuation Marks, Prepositional Phrases, & Other Phrases, Diagram Sentences that Seem Significant or Difficult

# of Verses	Level of Language Arts Proficiency (1-Beginner, 5-Expert)				
	1	2	3	4	5
31-50	Choose a Shorter Passage	Choose a Shorter Passage	Choose a Shorter Passage	Break the Passage at the Punctuation Marks	Break the Passage at Punctuation Marks
50+	Choose a Shorter Passage	Choose a Shorter Passage	Choose a Shorter Passage	Choose a Shorter Passage	Break the Passage at Punctuation Marks

Those who would like to get even more detailed about the structure of passages should consider diagraming all or some of the verses being studied. A quick Internet search will produce several sites that teach sentence diagramming.

Step Two: Find Key Words

One easy but very effective way to determine the structure of a passage is to look for key words in the passage. Once again, depending on your proficiency with English grammar, you can do take a simple approach, or you can take a more complicated approach. Let's start with a simple step that anyone can take.

Look for Repeated Words
If you like to write in books, or even if you don't, take a pen and underline the word "in" every time it shows up in Ephesians 1:3-14 below:

3 Blessed be the God and Father of our Lord Jesus Christ, who has blessed us in Christ with every spiritual blessing in the heavenly places, 4 even as he chose us in him before the foundation of the world, that we should be holy and blameless before him. In love 5 he predestined us for adoption to himself as sons through Jesus Christ, according to the purpose of his will, 6 to the praise of his glorious grace, with which he has blessed us in the Beloved. 7 In him we have redemption through his blood, the forgiveness of our trespasses, according to the riches of his grace, 8 which he lavished upon us, in all wisdom and insight 9 making known to us the mystery of his will, according to his purpose, which he set forth in Christ 10 as a plan for the fullness of time, to unite all things in him, things in heaven

and things on earth.**11** In him we have obtained an inheritance, having been predestined according to the purpose of him who works all things according to the counsel of his will,**12** so that we who were the first to hope in Christ might be to the praise of his glory. **13** In him you also, when you heard the word of truth, the gospel of your salvation, and believed in him, were sealed with the promised Holy Spirit, **14** who is the guarantee of our inheritance until we acquire possession of it, to the praise of his glory.

Whatever Paul, the author of Ephesians, is trying to tell us in this passage, he wants us to think about being "in." In what? Let's keep looking. Go back over the passage and circle every occurrence of "he," "him," or "his." Now, circle every word that refers to Jesus (Jesus, Christ, Beloved). Just noticing those three words and their relationship with one another reveals an important principle—our blessings come from being "in Christ."

Other Methods

Depending on your proficiency in English grammar, consider also completing the following analyses:

- Search for every verb in the passage. Verbs often control the thought and movement of a passage.
- Search for verbs by tense and type.
- Search the passage for first and second person pronouns and determine which ones are plural and which ones are singular (you may need the help of a Greek resource like Blue Letter Bible to determine when "you" is singular or plural).
- Look for synonyms in the passage.

All of these searches are designed to highlight key ideas that are communicated through repetition.

Let's apply these methods to Ephesians 1:20-21.

> *"That he worked in Christ when he raised him from the dead and seated him at his right hand in the heavenly places, far above all rule and authority and power and dominion, and above every name that is named, not only in this age but also in the one to come."*

Repeated Words in Ephesians 1:20-21
Because this is a shorter passage, there aren't as many repeated words as there were in Ephesians 1:3-14, but here are a few: "in" (x4), "him/his" (x3), "above" (x2).

Verbs in Ephesians 1:20-21
There are three verbs in this passage: worked, raised, and seated. Notice how the verbs are related. "Worked" is the main verb with "raised" and "seated" occurring in a prepositional phrase that describes the work.

Verbs by Tense and Type in Ephesians 1:20-21
All three verbs are past tense, active, indicative verbs.

First and Second Person Pronouns in Ephesians 1:20-21
There are no first or second person pronouns in this passage. While this might seem like it yields no important information, it actually is a good reminder that his passage is not about us! It is about "him" or Jesus.

Synonyms in Ephesians 1:20-21
While these are not exactly synonyms and their difference is important to understanding the passage, it is noteworthy that Paul lists several similar concepts back to back: rule, authority, power, dominion, and every name that is named.

This kind of analysis is very helpful for developing an outline. Let's combine all of our research into an organized flow of thought—an outline.

Step Three: Organizing the Ideas

Once you've broken the passage down and identified key words, the next step is to identify and organize the main ideas and supporting ideas. Let's use Ephesians 1:20-21 as an example. Looking as the most detailed breakdown above, *"That he worked"* is the only phrase to the far left. As a general rule, each level of an outline needs at least two points to justify having its own level. In this case, there seems to be one main idea—God worked—supported by several other ideas.

Because of the key word analyses, we also know that "worked" is the main verb in the passage and that "in" and "him/his" are the most repeated words. Since Jesus, or more specifically Christ, is the pronoun antecedent, the thesis of the passage is very clear: God's work in Christ. The thesis is best used as the title of the outline:

God's Work in Christ
1. Main Idea One
    a. Supporting Idea One
    b. Supporting Idea Two
2. Main Idea Two
    a. Supporting Idea One
    b. Supporting Idea Two

Remember, this is science *and* art, and breaking down the passage is a tool, not a law by which you must design your outline.

The main ideas are connected to the only two verbs remaining. God worked in Christ when He raised Him and seated Him.

God's Work in Christ
1. God raised Jesus from the dead.
    a. Supporting Idea One
    b. Supporting Idea Two
2. God seated Jesus in a position of honor.
    a. Supporting Idea One
    b. Supporting Idea Two

As we examine the text further, it appears there aren't any real supporting points for the first main idea, and that's alright; it just stands on its own, and Paul saw no need to clarify or develop the idea any further. If there aren't any sub points for a main idea, don't create some just to complete an outline. Let the point stand without any sub points. The second main idea, however, has several supporting points.

God's Work in Christ
1. God raised Jesus from the dead.
2. God seated Jesus in a position of honor.
    a. Jesus' position is at the right hand of God.
    b. Jesus' position is in the heavenly places.
    c. Jesus' position is above every other being's position.

This is a two level outline because it has points (level one) and sub points (level two). Several factors such as length of the passage, organization of the passage, your level of experience, etc. will determine how many levels each outline should have, but outlines more than three or four levels deep are probably not very effective.

Conclusion

Blueprints are vital for any significant construction project. They provide common points of reference to the builders, engineers, designers, landscapers and everyone else involved in the project. Blueprints help us visualize the final structure and see all the component parts on a few sheets of paper. Blueprints are great, but you can't walk into blueprints. You can't host a dinner party inside of a blueprint kitchen or have a family movie night in a blueprint living room. Blueprints are 2 dimensional representations of 3 dimensional realities incapable of revealing the full beauty, warmth, charm, and life of a structure.

Outlines can be like blueprints—2 dimensional representations of a passage, which is otherwise teeming with life. Now that you've learned how to Build an Outline and Find Key Words, return to the process of exploring the text. This time, we are going to invite some tour guides like commentators, scholars, and pastors to add a fresh perspective to the observations we've already made along the way and to help us answer some of our questions.

Learn to Love the **BIBLE:**

B-Begin with Prayer and Select a Passage
I- Inspect the Text:
      Read
      List Questions
      Make Observations
      Question the Text
      Consider the Literary Context
      Consider the Historical Context
B- Build an Outline
L-
E-

BUILD AN OUTLINE

Next Steps

Choose a few of the following passages, copy and paste them into a document, and follow the steps described in this chapter to create outlines:

Short
1.   Genesis 1:26-28
2.   Mark 1:9-11

Medium
3.   Hosea 3:1-5
4.   James 4:1-4

Long
5.   John 1:1-12
6.   Psalm 1
7.   Ephesians 2:1-10

8

LEARN FROM THE EXPERTS

"They received the word with all eagerness, examining the Scriptures daily to see if these things were so." Acts 17:11

"Milo Crinkley wanted to be perfect." So begins, *Be a Perfect Person in Just Three Days,* one of the most memorable books from my childhood. In the story, Milo comes across a book written by the fictional Dr. K. Pinkerton Silverfish with the same title in his school library, and inside, he found these precise instructions:

"Each evening you will read exactly one chapter of this book. You will follow my instructions precisely. At the end of the third day, you will be perfect, and I will congratulate you."

Following the instructions was a stern warning,

"BUT LET ME TELL YOU SOMETHING YOU'D BETTER NOT TRY. Under no circumstances should you attempt to become perfect in less than three days. Whatever you do, don't read more than one chapter each day. Many people are tempted to take a sneak look at the very last page before the third day is over. All I can say is, DON'T DO IT!"

Of course, Milo could not resist the temptation and turned to the last page only to find he had been outsmarted by Dr. Silverfish, who, anticipating the reader's lack of willpower, had written:

"BOY, ARE YOU DUMB! Didn't I tell you not to look at the last page of this book?"

After chiding the reader a bit more, Dr. Silverfish closed with these instructions:

"When you're ready to get serious about being perfect, open it to page ten. There you'll find instructions about what to do on day one of your program of perfection."[15]

DON'T READ THIS CHAPTER FIRST!

This is not a book about being perfect, but this is a book written with a process in mind—a process that is designed to help you grasp and act upon the meaning, implications, and applications of passages in the Bible. At the beginning of this book, there is a warning about jumping past the first part of the process and starting here, in this chapter. Some of you, however, are like Milo Crinkley, and you've ignored the warning. You are reading these words without having read anything else in the book because the title of this chapter seems most beneficial of them all. While I won't call you dumb, I will emphasize the importance of the process. There's a reason why you should BIB before you LE!

Now, if you're still with me, hopefully not because you ignored the warning, but because you've read the other chapters, let's get started. The process of Inspecting the Text and Building an Outline often creates more confusion than clarity, and that's one of the purposes of those steps. Without spending significant mental energy wrestling with the text, you might be able to learn a few facts about a passage, which you are likely to forget, but you'll never understand the passage in a truly satisfying way. Sure, anyone can read a commentary or listen to a

---

[15]. Stephen Manes, *Be a Perfect Person in Just Three Days!*, Reprint edition (Yearling, 1996).

sermon about a passage in the Bible, but one of the reasons you are reading this book is that you want to go deeper in your understanding of the Bible, and investing time and mental energy in the process is an important step.

FINALLY "THE EXPERTS"

By taking the first three steps, Begin with Prayer and Select a Passage, Inspect the Text, and Build an Outline, you've prepared your mind and heart to receive the message of the Bible. Now, investing your time and energy listening to experts will pay off.

Three Important Questions

There are three important questions to ask about using scholars to help you understand the Bible. What kinds of resources are best? Which resources can be trusted? What is the best way to use resources? Let's start with the first question.

What Kinds of Resources are Best?

There are many, many types of resources that might be helpful for correcting and expanding your list of observations and answering some of the questions you've raised in your preliminary work. First, let's consider Bible Commentaries.

Using Bible Commentaries

While there are many resources available for Bible study, commentaries are the bread and butter of biblical interpretation. Commentaries are books which offer comments on each verse of a book or section of the Bible.

Devotional, Pastoral, and Technical Commentaries

Commentaries range in scope from those written for devotional purposes to those written for serious academic study dealing with very technical issues. Each type can be helpful depending on your goals and level of experience studying the Bible. While commentaries are often described using other adjectives (critical, homiletical, academic, exegetical, sermonic), those adjectives are synonymous with one of the three descriptors I have chosen to use in this section, and reading just a few sentences of most commentaries will quickly reveal which category best describes the resource.

Devotional. Devotional commentaries are written to inspire and encourage, so they often focus on application rather than exegesis (exploring the passage carefully to understand its meaning). Consider this excerpt from a devotional commentary on Galatians 3:15:

> "Paul began this section by addressing his readers as 'brethren.' Though he passionately disagreed with their beliefs and practices, he did not use insulting or demeaning language. Even Christians who disagree can relate courteously to one another."[16]

Notice how the author focuses on the implications of Paul's use of the word "brethren" and very quickly moves to apply that implication to all Christians.

Technical. Technical commentaries frequently use the original languages (Hebrew, Aramaic, and Greek) without translating them. They are written to the academic community and assume the reader has the knowledge of a seminary student. Another distinguishing mark of a technical commentary is that they usually employ a different author for each book of the Bible. Many devotional or pastoral commentaries (though not all of them) are written by a single author and cover the New Testament, the Old Testament, or even the entire Bible; technical commentaries will not take that approach because no one is enough of an expert to adequately exegete more than a few books of the Bible at the technical commentary level of difficulty. Here's an excerpt from a technical commentary on the same verse from Galatians:

> "On Paul's affectionate use of 'brothers' in such a severe letter as Galatians, see *Comment* at 1:11. The vocative αδελφοί appears almost always in Galatians at the epistolary seams: at the start of a major section (1:11; 4:12; 5:13), at the start of a subunit within a section (here; 6:1), at the end of a unit of material (4:31; 5:11), or as the final word of the entire letter (6:18, not counting ἀμήν). So except for its use at 4:28, αδελφοί functions

---

[16]. Thomas Lea, *Galatians: Saved By Grace* (Convention Press, 1994) pg. 52

as an epistolary convention by signalling certain breaks in the letter structure of Galatians, as well as expressing Paul's sincere affection."[17]

These two examples represent the ends of the scale. One barely focuses on the actual wording of the text and immediately begins to draw out implications and applications, while the other focuses solely on Paul's pattern of usage for the Greek word, translated, 'brothers.'

Pastoral. Between the devotional and technical commentaries are those often described as pastoral. These commentaries read like well-crafted sermons with a mixture of technical exegesis and devotional application. They sometimes deal with the original languages, but do so in a way that is accessible to those who haven't studied them. In the first two examples, commentators discussed the word "brothers" from Galatians 3:15—first with a devotional approach and second with a technical approach. To understand the pastoral approach, compare those examples with the discussion below of "covenant," another word from Galatians 3:15, from a pastoral commentary:

> "Diatheke (covenant) is a general term for a binding agreement. It was often used to refer to wills or testaments, and in some Scripture passages the word is best translated with that meaning. A last will and testament expresses the desires and intent of but one party and may or may not involve other specific parties. A covenant, on the other hand, always involves two or more specific parties, although the terms may be stipulated and fulfilled by only one. In the Septuagint (the Greek Old Testament translated in the 3rd century B.C.), the term is consistently used of God's covenants with His people—covenants that God alone initiated and established and that sometimes were conditional and sometimes were not."[18]

---

[17]. Richard N. Longenecker, *Word Biblical Commentary Vol. 41, Galatians*, Word Biblical Commentary edition (Dallas, Tex.: Thomas Nelson, 1990) pg. 126

[18]. John F. MacArthur Jr, *The Macarthur New Testament Commentary: Galatians*, First Edition (Chicago: Moody Publishers, 1987) pg. 83

Notice that, like the technical commentary, this commentary deals with a Greek word, but the word is spelled out with English letters instead of Greek letters and is translated and illustrated for the reader. There's no need to have any knowledge of Greek in order to understand the author's point.

Depending on the style of the author, pastoral commentaries can be more devotional or more technical, but the distinguishing characteristic is that they are organized and written like a sermon; in fact, many pastoral commentaries are developed by editing transcribed sermons.

Table 6: Types of Commentaries

Type	Devotional	Pastoral	Technical
Purpose	Inspiration	Instruction	Information
Difficulty	Easy	Medium	Challenging
Biblical Languages?	None	Yes, but with no technical skills needed	Yes, basic language skills assumed
Uses	Daily devotional, encouragement, applying a passage	Understanding and applying the basic meaning of a passage	Academic research, studying difficult passages

What Level is Right for Me? Many of you, especially those who are new to studying the Bible, might assume that devotional commentaries are the best place to start, but I don't think that's a good idea. Devotional commentaries play an important role, but they include too much of the author's opinions and too little reliance on the history of interpretation. Please see appendix 3 for more information on the history of interpretation.

My advice is that you use the pastoral commentaries like travelers use interstates. They will be the most effective routes to understanding the basic meaning of the text, and they should be where most Bible students spend the majority of their time. Devotional commentaries will be like scenic byways meandering through the mountains, offering beautiful scenery without necessarily covering that much distance. Technical commentaries, to follow the metaphor, are like the streets and avenues of a city. Once travelers exit an interstate, they get a much better feel for the details, but their journey becomes much slower and more difficult. I often read the pastoral commentaries first then turn to the technical commentaries to answer remaining questions or explore particular verses or phrases in more detail. Finally, to make sure I'm connecting the idea to the real experiences of those I'm trying to reach and disciple, I read devotional commentaries.

We Must Read Old Commentaries

CS Lewis famously advised those of his day to read books from another time. He said,

> "Every age has its own outlook. It is specially good at seeing certain truths and specially liable to make certain mistakes. We all, therefore, need the books that will correct the characteristic mistakes of our own period. And that means the old books."[19]

And, if I might add, that means the old commentaries! Many of the giants of the faith wrote commentaries—Augustine, Calvin, Luther, Spurgeon, Edwards—and many of them are available for free online. As you study the Bible, you'll find references to other commentators and their works from Christian history—find and use those too.

Don't Miss This One!

I'll admit that I'm showing my bias here, but I don't want you to miss out. In the early years of the 18th century, an English minister compiled devotional thoughts on the entire Bible and began to publish them. Through that work, Matthew Henry has influenced Christians of every subsequent generation. Henry is often called the Prince of Commentators, and his work still speaks clearly and affectively to the hearts and minds of Christ's followers in the 21st century. Don't miss Matthew Henry. His work is best categorized as a pastoral commentary although it has characteristics of a devotional commentary. However the work is classified, it is filled with wisdom and insight, which

---

[19]. "Detroit Baptist Theological Seminary - C. S. Lewis on Reading Old Books," accessed November 21, 2016, http://www.dbts.edu/2013/01/15/c-s-lewis-on-reading-old-books/.

challenges and encourages the reader. The original was written in archaic English, but updated versions are available in many formats.

Other Resources

In addition to commentaries, there are other great sources for studying the Bible. Once you've started the study process through your own work and through reliable commentaries, you'll be able to recognize good resources from bad resources. Then, you can safely utilize resources like those mentioned below.

Sermons and Lectures

Most pastors make their sermons available in audio and/or video format through a podcast or website, and they are often cataloged by Bible book, chapter, and verse(s). For instance, John Macarthur has preached through every verse of the New Testament, and those audio sermons are available at www.gty.org. Many historically significant sermons have been preserved for us in written form and published in collections of sermons. I have a copy of Spurgeon's sermons, and the set includes a Scripture index, which lists the pages that discuss particular verses of Scripture to guide me to sermons discussing the passages I'm studying.

Lectures can also be very helpful. They are more technical than sermons, but they aren't as hard to understand as some technical commentaries. Several seminaries and Bible colleges, such as Reformed Theological Seminary and Liberty University, post their audio lectures online and through a service called iTunesU available in the iTunes store. Those lectures include overviews of each book of the Bible and lectures on difficult passages and topics.

Earlier, we discussed the importance of developing a good systematic theology through which to view all of Scripture, and there are great resources to develop a strong systematic theology. Several trusted authors have produced systematic theologies, and your pastor should be able to recommend which particular resource would be best for you. Wayne Grudem, a noted author and theologian, produced audio lectures on each chapter of his monumental work, Systematic Theology, and they are available at www.monergism.com/systematic-theology-mp3-lecture-series. You will certainly benefit from those.

Internet Resources

Let's be real. These other resources are great, but when we have a question, we google it, and that's okay. It's a gift of God's grace that we have access to so much information and so many resources. In fact, there are many great resources available on the Internet for understanding the Bible. Unfortunately, there are many dangerous resources available on the Internet that use small amounts of truth to teach dangerous and destructive doctrines. BEWARE! This might sound counter-intuitive, but I recommend that you avoid Internet resources when you are first beginning to study the Bible. That is, of course, unless you are wisely using the Internet to access some of the resources already mentioned; remember that many commentaries have online versions.

Once you begin to use the Internet for study, make sure you read the web address for the site you're planning to visit. For instance, if the web address has JW or LDS in it, those are likely Jehovah Witness or Mormon (Later Day Saints) websites and should be avoided. Also, read the "About" section for the groups and/or beliefs connected with the site. Finally, ask your pastor or trusted Christian friends which sites they use, and send them links of sites you are thinking of using.

As of the writing of this book, here are a few websites that I use and recommend:
* www.blueletterbible.org
* www.biblestudytools.com/csb/
* www.soniclight.com
* www.monergism.com
* www.desiringgod.org
* resources.thegospelcoalition.org

Human Resources

Ideas don't come from books. Ideas come from humans, and for every commentary, there are hundreds of pastors and Bible scholars who will never write a commentary. As you study the Bible, ask your pastor to help you with difficult passages. Also, consider contacting the biblical studies professors from trusted, conservative seminaries. Most of them have email addresses listed on the school's website, and they are often willing to help. I've emailed professors on several occasions, and many of them have responded with recommended articles, books, or other resources.

Which Resources Can be Trusted?

Not all resources are created equally, so how can you know which resources to trust? Let me suggest a few sources:

- Your pastor and church library—If you attend a church that teaches the Bible authoritatively and exegetically (revealing the plain truth of the passage), this is the best place to start. Your pastor might even let you borrow some of his books.
- Local theological libraries—if you live close to a trusted Bible college or seminary, find out if you can use their library. The commentaries on their shelves have likely been evaluated for quality and doctrine.
- As of the writing of this book, bestcommentaries.com is the best online resource I've found for commentary recommendations.
- The site referenced in an earlier chapter, blueletterbible.org, includes several resources on each verse of Scripture in its resource tabs. Just remember to search for the passage first, then click on the "Tools" button.
- Use your human resources by emailing seminary professors, pastors, and other trusted sources to ask which websites, podcasts, pastors, etc. they recommend.

What is the Best Way to Use Resources?

To make the most of the resources available to you, determine a time, place, and method for using resources other than the Bible.

Time

I'm not a mind reader, but the chances are really good that many of you are thinking, "Time! Where can I find some of that?" We live in a society that is obsessed with being busy. In fact, we often substitute business for productivity, but that's a subject for another occasion. The truth is that we all have more time than we think we have, and we will never find the time to do what we really want to do if we don't sacrifice some lesser things. You probably won't find any time to study the Bible without making significant changes to your schedule, so here are a few tips on how to make better use of your time:

- Be deliberate about your study time. Plan it, put it on the calendar, and don't skip it! Treat it like an important doctor's appointment.
- Talk with your family or friends about finding time to study the Bible. You might be surprised at their insights and willingness to help.
- Consider getting up earlier. I know—it's hard, but normally the only barrier you have to overcome is yourself, and that makes the early morning the easiest place to find more time. A good verse for encouragement is Mark 1:35, which says of Jesus, "*And rising very early in the morning, while it was still dark, he departed and went out to a desolate place, and there he prayed.*"
- Remove time killers. Most television shows require a 1-hour investment, and honestly, the return on investment is not very high. Consider replacing TV with study of Scripture; and then there's Social Media. John Piper has prophetically quipped, "One of the great uses of Twitter and Facebook will be to prove at the Last Day that prayerlessness was not from lack of time." We could say the same thing about lack of Bible study.
- Turn off your phone. This is another time killer, but it deserves its own bullet point. Since the invention of smartphones, we rarely experience boredom. How much more time would you have if you turned off your phone for an hour each day? If that seems impossible, just consider what would happen if you lost your phone—the world would still turn, and everything would proceed as it has since the beginning of time. If someone gets mad because you didn't answer their call or text them immediately, just tell them you were listening to Jesus, and encourage them to take their complaints directly to Him!
- Determine how much time you plan to study, set a timer and study for the pre-determined amount of time unless an emergency arises. Reward yourself with a piece of chocolate or something similar each time you complete the study time.

Place

Where you will study is just as important as when you will study. Ideally, your study place will have the three P's (in order of importance): peace, permanence, and plenty of space. The best study places are quiet and calm places, where resources, notes, pens, etc. can be spread out and left out without being disturbed or causing the house, room or building to appear cluttered. A corner table or roll top desk will work well.

If you can't find a table in a peaceful place that is conducive for leaving books open and notes spread out, consider creative ways to find peace and permanence. For instance, a well-organized book bag dedicated just for Bible study can provide a type of permanence. Keep all your resources and notes in the bag, using folders and bookmarks as needed, so the resources can be removed and spread out quickly to recreate your last study layout. For peace, consider using a white noise app with headphones—several versions are available for free, and they provide background noise, which drowns out other distracting noises, allowing you to focus.

Method

You've picked out a place with the three P's, you've set aside time and removed all distractions—so now what? What do you actually do when using resources to study the Bible? While there's no one correct method, here's what I do: I spend a few minutes organizing my resources. For books, I stack them in order with the ones I think will be most helpful on top and those I think might be least helpful on bottom (I'm almost always wrong about that, by the way!). For electronic resources, I bring them up in different tabs on my Internet browser in order of perceived importance. Then, with my Bible open and my questions, observations, and outline nearby, I start reading. As I read the pertinent sections of one resource, I move it to the side and read the next, making notes as I read. Inevitably, I run out of time before I run out of resources, but I leave with a much greater understanding of the passage. My method is just that—my method. It works for me, but it might not work for you. Experiment with different methods and strategies until you find one that works best for you, but make sure your study always includes an open Bible, your questions and observations, and a notebook or electronic document in which you can take notes.

Organizing Electronic Study Notes and Files

In previous generations, entire books were written about developing effective systems for filing paper work. Thanks to personal computers, that need no longer exists. Now, we store important information in computer files, and I suppose most of you will store your study notes there as well. So, instead of an entire book about filing strategies, a paragraph or two should suffice.

The most important aspect of an electronic filing system is that you back it up. With the advent of cloud computing, there are many different options for doing so—most of us won't fail to back up our work because of a lack of options; we fail because of a lack of discipline. You can bemoan your lack of discipline hoping to one day be better at backing up your files, or you can use a system which automatically backs up important documents. That's what I do!

The second important characteristic of an electronic filing system is organization. The best way to organize electronic files of Bible study notes is by book, verse, and chapter. Here's a simple system that has been helpful for me:

1. Inside of a folder named Bible Study Notes, create two folders named 01[20]_Old Testament and 02_New Testament.
2. Inside each of those folders, create one folder for each book of that testament, and name them according to the following pattern: For the Old Testament, 01_Genesis, 02_Exodus . . . 11_1 Kings, 12_2 Kings . . . 23_Isaiah . . . 39_Malachi and for the New Testament, 01_Matthew, 02_Mark . . . 27_Revelation. Even if you don't create a folder for each book right away, create folders for the books you are studying and make sure to number the folders you create according to their position in the testament.
3. As you study, name the files containing your notes in this pattern: chapter number_number of first verse studied. For instance, study notes on Jeremiah 14:1-5 would be saved as 14_1 and placed in the Jeremiah folder.

---

[20]. If you don't use the numbering system, your computer will organize the files according to alphabetical order. Numbers allow you to control the order of the files. Adding a 0 to files 1-9 is important because computers organize by the value of the first character and will therefore put a file name 11_ ahead of a file named 6_ because 6 is larger than 1.

This method organizes your files in the same order as Scripture, which will make your files much easier to access.

Conclusion

A friend of mine works in construction and, recently, his company was remodeling a house that needed a new coat of stucco on the exterior, so they hired a subcontractor to handle the job. Despite the stucco company spending thousands of dollars in materials and dozens of man-hours coating the house with stucco, when my friend arrived at the jobsite the next day, all of the stucco was laying on the ground—it had all fallen off, and the job was a complete loss! What happened? The surface wasn't properly prepared, and there was a layer of dirt and grime on the wall, so the stucco didn't stick to the wall. For round two, my friend hired a different company who scraped, cleaned, and pressure washed the surface thoroughly to provide a good surface for the stucco. What's the lesson? It doesn't matter how much time and money you spend if you don't prepare the surface and use the right experts!

You've prepared your mind by taking the first three steps, and now, by learning from the experts, you've applied additional insights that you'll understand and remember. In this process, you will also come to see the beauty of God's Word even more.

Learn to Love the **BIBLE**:

B-Begin with Prayer and Select a Passage
I- Inspect the Text:
Read
List Questions
Make Observations
Question the Text
Consider the Literary Context
Consider the Historical Context
B- Build an Outline
L- Learn from Experts
E-

Next Steps

1. Look for resources by visiting some of the websites mentioned in this chapter, asking if your church or pastor has a library that you can access, and looking for local Bible colleges and seminaries that might give you access to their libraries for study. Be sure to check with your pastor about the trustworthiness of the college or seminary.
2. Gather the resources you've found in a designated study place and set aside an hour or more to study those resources, frequently referring back to the Bible and your list of questions and observations.
3. Review your list of questions to determine if all of them have been answered. If not, look for other resources to address remaining questions.
4. Keep a journal (written or electronic) with the key insights you learn from your study and share them with a friend.
5. Use one of your designated study times to create an electronic filing system as described in this chapter.

9

END WITH APPLICATION

"But be doers of the word, and not hearers only, deceiving yourselves. For if anyone is a hearer of the word and not a doer, he is like a man who looks intently at his natural face in a mirror. For he looks at himself and goes away and at once forgets what he was like. But the one who looks into the perfect law, the law of liberty, and perseveres, being no hearer who forgets but a doer who acts, he will be blessed in his doing." James 1:22-25

I recently read that the average millennial will take 25,700 selfies over the course of a lifetime. 25,700 selfies! It's my uneducated guess that about 25,000 of those will be deleted in hopes of a better selfie, but that's still a lot of pictures. In light of the selfie world we now inhabit, can you imagine grabbing a smartphone, extending your arm into the sky, titling your head just right, smiling just enough but not too much, and snapping a great selfie only to find, upon reviewing the selfie, that you have a big piece of lettuce stuck in your teeth? What would you do? James 1:22-25 says that those who learn what the Bible says but don't make any changes to their lives are like people who see themselves but forget what they look like. In other words, instead of getting the piece of lettuce out of your teeth, you forget it's there and post the lettuce tooth selfie to social media!

James is right. It would be absolutely foolish to study the Bible without applying the truths we've learned to our lives, and this chapter will help you develop a plan for applying the truths you've learned.

There are two steps to creating an application plan: 1) summarizing what you've learned, and 2) determining what actions to take based on what you've learned.

Step One: Summarize What You've Learned

Following the process laid out in this book, has taken you on a journey during which you've learned and experienced so much about the passage you've been studying. If you're going to follow the command of James 1:22, it's vital to summarize what you've learned. The best counseling sessions uncover and explore many areas, but they also end with clear takeaways and action steps. The same is true for studying the Bible. How can we create takeaways and action steps after studying the Bible so deeply and intentionally? Ask more questions!

Three Summary Questions

With your Bible open and your notes in front of you, prayerfully ask these three questions, in this order: What does this teach me about God? What does this teach me about humanity? What does this teach me about myself? Now here's the hard part—limit your answers to one or two sentences per question that concisely capture the essence of what you've learned.

Asking the questions in order will give proper focus to your summary; remember the Bible is primarily a book about God, not a book about you or me. Everything the Bible has to say about us, it says in relation to what it first says about God and also what it says about all of humanity. Without intentionally thinking in this order, we will naturally focus on ourselves to the exclusion of God and others.

Limiting the answers to one or two sentences will force you to think about the big picture, which is important since you've spent most of your time inspecting the text carefully. We need to study the trees to help us understand the forest, but we can't forget the forest!

Find a distinct place in your notes to write out the application process, and start by answering the three questions. Although this process will look very different for each person and passage, here's an example of possible answers to the three summary questions from Ephesians chapter 1.

1. What does this passage teach me about God? *God is one God in three persons, Father, Son, and Spirit, who is glorified through the preordained salvation of those in Christ. He is loving, powerful, and gracious, and He displays all of that through salvation.*
2. What does this passage teach me about humanity? *Every person is either in Christ or not in Christ. Those who are in Christ receive every spiritual blessing available.*
3. What does this passage teach me about myself? *Because I am in Christ, I have been predestined, chosen, and adopted as a child of God to receive every spiritual blessing through Christ, and I have been sealed with the Holy Spirit as a guarantee. As I grow spiritually, I will come to understand the blessings I have more and more, and I will understand how the power of God is at work in my life.*

The Gospel Question

Now that you've summarized what the passage teaches about God, humanity, and yourself, end step one by asking the gospel question. The gospel question is not actually a single question, but rather a set of questions that answers a single question, "What does this passage have to do with the person and work of Jesus?"

Charles Spurgeon, the beloved 19th century British preacher famously described his method for preparing sermons this way, "I take my text and make a bee-line to the cross."[21] The reason Spurgeon could so adamantly promote and practice such a strategy for preaching is that every passage in the Bible, from Genesis 1:1 to Revelation 22:21, is connected directly to the person and work of Jesus.

There is no single question that will always reveal the connection between a passage and the gospel, but here are a few that might help.

---

[21]. Lewis Drummond, "Spurgeon, Prince of Preachers" 223

Old Testament Passages

- If the event recorded in this passage had never occurred, would Jesus have been born?
- Does this passage describe something that the New Testament identifies as a foreshadowing of Jesus and His death, burial, and/or resurrection?
- Does this passage discuss the holiness of God or the seriousness of humanity's sin, which are the two conflicting forces addressed at the cross?
- Does this passage record the account of an Old Testament hero who has characteristics of the perfect leader/king/ruler, but ultimately fails to be that pointing to the need for Jesus as our perfect ruler?

New Testament Passages

- Does this passage record events from the life of Jesus?
- How would the message of this passage be affected if Jesus never lived, or if He was never crucified and resurrected?
- Does this passage instruct me to live a righteous life that I know I cannot live so that my only hope is to be forgiven by Jesus and empowered by Him?
- Does this passage instruct me to place my ultimate hope in Jesus and not the world?
- Does this passage instruct me to love, forgive, or be patient, kind, etc. to people who don't necessarily deserve that kind of treatment from me, so that the only way I can live this out is by following the example of Jesus, who loved me and gave Himself for me while I was still a rebellious sinner not deserving of His love?

Jesus, His person, and His life, death, burial, and resurrection stand as the central theme of all Scripture. If we properly understand the context and direct, immediate meaning of a Bible passage, but we fail to see its connection to the cross, we would have been just as well off to have never read the passage.

What does the gospel have to do with application? Everything! As we study the Bible, it's important to see the gospel woven into every passage for two reasons. First, it gives us a chance to preach the gospel to ourselves, and we need to be reminded over and over again that our salvation only comes through the work of Jesus on the cross. We were enemies of God because of our sin—our rebellion against God—but God loved us while we were still His enemies, and He sent His Son, Jesus, to take the punishment for our sin by dying on the cross and to defeat death, hell, and the grave by being raised from the dead. Now, everyone who turns from sin and trusts Jesus as Savior and Lord receives forgiveness and eternal life. It was Martin Luther who first encouraged Christians to "Preach the gospel to yourself everyday."[22] As we see the gospel in the passage we study, we can preach the gospel to ourselves—there is no greater application than this.

Second, seeing the gospel in every passage we study teaches us about the nature of the Christian life. Every subject in the Bible from the deeply theological ones, like salvation, to the extremely practical ones, like marriage and parenting, is based on the gospel. As we learn to see the gospel in every passage, we will develop a deeper understanding of how the gospel is THE central message of the Bible, and we will have a much better foundation for living out all the practical steps given in the Bible.

As you ask the gospel question, summarize your answer in one or two sentences and add it to your notes with the answers to the previous three summary questions.

Here's an example from Ephesians 1:

4. What does this passage have to do with the person and work of Jesus? *The blessings of Ephesians 1 are for those in Christ, and it's only through the work of Jesus on the cross and His resurrection that those blessings are available to anyone. The power working for my salvation is the same power that God used when He raised Jesus from the dead and seated Him in the heavenly places.*

Step Two: Determine Actions Steps

Now, having explored a passage thoroughly and with a good summary of what God has taught you through His Word, you are fully prepared to act on what you've learned. The entire BIBLE process is about asking questions, so it shouldn't be a surprise that developing action steps starts by asking a question, "What is the proper response to what

---

[22]. http://www.ligonier.org/learn/articles/seeing-gospel-word-god/

God has shown me in His Word?" Perhaps you need to repent of sinful behavior that has been revealed. Maybe you need to start a new habit of spiritual discipline or memorize a key verse, or verses, or chapter of Scripture; and of course, there will always be thought processes that need to change. Remember to make this a prayerful process and be really sensitive to the leading of God through the Holy Spirit. Sometimes the action steps will be radical, and sometimes they will be subtle. Most often, you'll develop 3-5 action steps, but make sure you stay open to whatever God reveals to you. When it comes to God's leading to change according to His will, refuse to refuse.

Action steps should be listed in your notes just below your summary questions and statements. If you are using an electronic document to take notes, consider starting a new page to record the summary statements and action steps. Based on previous study in Ephesians 1, here are a few application points.

Action Step 1: Pray intentionally for my spiritual growth, and the spiritual growth of my wife and three other friends every day for one week using the wording of Ephesians 1:16-19.

Action Step 2: Set aside 30 minutes on Wednesday morning next week to read Ephesians 1, worship God, and praise Him for the salvation of those who are in Christ.

Action Step 3: Memorize Ephesians 1:3-7 next week and share it with a prayer partner or spouse.

Conclusion

You did it! You stayed with the process, and now, 1) you've learn so much about the passage you studied, and 2) you've developed the skills that will help you study any passage of the Bible in the future. So now what? Start the process again with another passage. The more you practice, the more these steps will merge, and the more adept you'll become at determining which steps need more focus and attention for a given passage and which steps aren't as helpful to you as you learn to love God's Word.

Learn to Love the **BIBLE**:

B-Begin with Prayer and Select a Passage
I- Inspect the Text:
       Read
       List Questions
       Make Observations
       Question the Text
       Consider the Literary Context
       Consider the Historical Context
B- Build an Outline
L- Learn from Experts
E- End with Application

Next Steps

1. Using the passage you've been studying, apply the two-step application process to develop 3-5 action steps.
2. After you've developed the actions steps, ask a friend to hold you accountable by meeting with you to listen to your summaries and action steps. Plan a second meeting with the same friend where you can update him or her on your progress.
3. Share what you've learned with others. Find one follower of Christ and one person who does not follow Jesus, and share what you've learned with them.

Which Translation Should I Use?

A good translation is an important tool for studying and loving the Bible, but there are so many to choose from! If you are new to studying the Bible, then you might feel lost when trying to choose a translation. In fact, you might not even know what I'm talking about.

Although the Bible was originally written in Hebrew, Aramaic, and Greek, it has been translated for us by many different people and groups over the centuries. Contrary to what some people think, this doesn't mean the Bible has lost its meaning, because modern translators do not use old translations; they use ancient manuscripts written in the original languages. In other words, each translation does not inherit the potential mistakes of previous translations because they use Hebrew, Aramaic, and Greek manuscripts instead of other translations when they are doing their work. These translations go by different names and abbreviations like the King James Version (KJV), the New International Version (NIV), the Holman Christian Standard Bible (HCSB), etc. If you are not sure which translation you have, look on the cover or the title page.

Why are there so Many Translations?

They are trying to change the Bible! Not really, but that's what some people think. In short, the main reason there are so many translations is not that the Bible has changed—it's that English keeps changing. Think of all the people throughout history and throughout the modern world who use the English language. No single English translation can meet all the needs of all English speakers in all parts of the world throughout all of history.

One of my favorite examples comes from the Song of Solomon 5:4, which describes the elation of a woman when she realized her boyfriend was coming to visit her. The King James Version, one of the earliest English translations of the Bible, describes her feelings this way, "my bowels were moved for him." It gets me every time! Imagine telling your sweetie, "Honey, I love you so much you make my bowels move!" That might have sounded romantic in the 17th century, but it means something very different now. Other translations use more modern idioms that are still true to the meaning of the Hebrew expression. For instance, the English Standard Version says, "My heart was thrilled within me." The Hebrew word used in Song of Solomon 5:4 refers to all of the internal organs and can specifically refer to the seat of human emotions, wherein its context seems to indicate is its use here. So in the 17th century, "bowels" might have made more sense, but in 21st century English, "heart" is much more accurate to the meaning of the text. In short, if you are going to buy a Valentine's card that quotes Song of Solomon 5:4, make sure you check the version first!

What are the Major Differences Between Translations?

So, which translation should you use? That depends on your personal needs. While there is no perfect translation, there are some important differences. Most of this information is available in the preface of each translation or on the publisher's website.

The Manuscripts Used

The Bible was originally written in three languages: Hebrew, Aramaic, and Greek. Virtually all versions of the Bible translate from these languages directly into English, Spanish, Mandarin, etc. In other words, contrary to what many people believe, scholars are not that far removed from the original writings. In most cases, they are using manuscripts (hand written copies that descended directly from the original writings), which the science of textual criticism has shown to be very close to the originals.

Translations can be separated into two categories: those translated from the Erasmus Text, also known as the Textus Receptus, and those translated from modern Greek texts, which are compiled from all of the currently available manuscripts. All translations basically use the same text to translate the Old Testament called the Masoretic Text, so the differences are all in the New Testament.

The Erasmus Text

In the 16th century, a man named Erasmus compiled and printed a copy of the Greek New Testament using all of the Greek manuscripts he could gather, mostly dated from the 12th century (about 1,000 years after the last book of the Bible was written). During the Reformation and for many years afterwards, the Erasmus text was the most widely used version of the Greek New Testament. Even now, there are several versions that are translated from the Erasmus Text including the King James Version, the New King James Version, and the Modern English Version.

Most contemporary people who use the Erasmus Text believe that it is the only accurate Greek New Testament. If you have ever heard that the King James Bible is the only accurate translation, its translation from the Erasmus Text is the basis for that argument. Most modern scholars, including most evangelical scholars and conservative scholars, reject that argument. While recognizing the Erasmus Text as a very important historical achievement that supported translation work for over two centuries, most scholars prefer modern Greek texts.

Modern Greek Texts

Most translations use a modern Greek New Testament like the United Bible Society's Greek New Testament. These Greek texts use all available Greek manuscripts, many of which have been discovered since Erasmus compiled his Greek New Testament and are much older, with some dating to the 2nd century AD (less than 100 years after the last book of the Bible was written). Through a careful process called textual criticism, these Greek texts attempt to uncover and correct errors resulting from the copying process, and the variant readings are included as footnotes.

One of the most amazing facts that supports the trustworthiness of God's Word is the similarity of the Erasmus Text and modern Greek texts. Despite different philosophies and strategies, and despite some sections that contain significant differences (like the short ending of Mark or the absence of John 7:53-8:11), modern Greek texts and the Erasmus text agree about 98% of the time.

The Goals and Philosophy of the Translation Committees

Every team of translators has different reasons for creating a new translation. Most translators have a target audience they are trying to reach, which impacts their translation strategy. Some translations are produced for theological reasons like correcting perceived errors of earlier translators, and some are produced for more practical reasons such as avoiding copyright issues. Many translations are produced just to provide a fresh reading of Scripture or to keep up with changes in the English language. The good news is most translations include a preface, which explains their goals and strategies.

Word for Word or Thought for Thought

One major strategic decision every translations team must make is the choice between a word for word strategy (often called formal equivalence) and a thought for thought strategy (often called dynamic equivalence). In other words, the translators must decide if they will translate each Hebrew, Aramaic, or Greek word into the corresponding English word or if they will try to capture each complete thought expressed in Hebrew, Aramaic, or Greek and translate those into corresponding complete thoughts in the English language.

At first, it seems like a word for word translation is best, but anyone fluent in multiple languages knows that literal, word for word translations are sometimes inaccurate. Then again, at certain times, a terse accuracy comes from a word to word translation that gets lost with thought for thought translations. Furthermore, a thought for thought strategy assumes the translators accurately know the thoughts expressed in the original languages.

A Spectrum of Strategies

Most translations are neither completely formal equivalence translations nor dynamic equivalence translations, but instead fall somewhere on a spectrum between the two extremes. A quick Internet search will produce a myriad of charts and diagrams that place translations on a scale, and most translations discuss their approach in the preface. Generally speaking, the more easy to read and modern a Bible sounds, the more its translators used a thought for thought strategy, and the more terse and formal a Bible sounds, the more its translators used a word for word strategy.

Which Translation is Most Accurate?

If one translation was clearly more accurate than all the others, this entire section on translations could be one sentence long—"The most accurate translation is the _____." But, of course, it's just not that simple. There are so many factors contributing to accuracy that it's impossible to name one single translation as "most accurate." Finding a very accurate translation, however, is not a hopeless task. If you ask scholars, professors, and pastors what they consider the most accurate translation, you will likely hear three or four answers over and over again— the English Standard Version, the King James Version, the New American Standard Bible, the New King James Version, and some obscure version none of us has ever heard of! If you use one of those translations as your primary Bible, you are in good shape.

What Factors Other than Accuracy Should I Consider?

This section could really be titled, "What does accuracy mean anyway?" Every translation has some level of inaccuracy because it changes the original Hebrew, Greek, or Aramaic words and syntax into words and syntax that are not Hebrew, Greek, or Aramaic! In other words, the only way to read a completely accurate version of the Bible is to read the Bible in its original languages. Since most Christians cannot do that, we need translations, which put the Hebrew, Greek, and Aramaic words and syntax into English words and syntax we can understand. So, I suggest that your translation is only accurate if you can understand it. Otherwise, if you read English words you don't understand, you might as well read Hebrew, Greek, and Aramaic words you don't understand.

Here are four rules to follow when choosing a translation for reading and studying:
- Choose more than one translation. The translation you read might not be the translation you study. Or, if you read through the Bible each year, you might choose a different translation each year. Certainly when you are studying, you should reference several translations. By using a variety of translations, you will get the benefit of all of them and understand passages in a new light.
- If you are not a great reader, choose a translation that you can understand, but that also challenges your reading skills. In other words, it needs to be readable but challenging. This helps ensure accuracy, while also developing your skills as a reader.
- Use translations recommended or used by conservative, Bible teaching pastors whose sermons reveal a high view of Scripture. Such translations include, but are not limited to, the English Standard Version, the Holman Christian Standard Bible, the King

James Version, the New American Standard Bible, the New
International Version, and the New King James Version.
- Use the Internet to test drive a translation before purchasing a new
Bible, and ask trusted pastors if they recommend the translation.

What is a Paraphrase?

According to etomonline.com, paraphrase means, "to tell in other
words." It comes from two Greek words that mean to tell beside or
alongside. Think of parallel lines. They are not the same, but they are in
the same plane and are heading in the same direction. In the same way,
a paraphrase tells the same story and heads in the same direction as a
translation of Scripture, but it moves a little closer to the culture than a
translation can while maintaining the accuracy of a translation. To
understand the difference, compare Psalm 23:1-3 in the KJV, the ESV,
and the Message (a paraphrase).

KJV
The Lord is my shepherd; I shall not want. He maketh me to lie down
in green pastures: he leadeth me beside the still waters. He restoreth my
soul: he leadeth me in the paths of righteousness for his name's sake.

ESV
The Lord is my shepherd; I shall not want. He makes me lie down in
green pastures.
He leads me beside still waters. He restores my soul. He leads me
in paths of righteousness for his name's sake.

The Message
God, my shepherd! I don't need a thing. You have bedded me down in
lush meadows, you find me quiet pools to drink from. True to your
word, you let me catch my breath and send me in the right direction.

The Message, a paraphrase, is similar to the KJV and ESV translations,
but it is on a slightly different track.

Paraphrases can be very helpful devotional and even study tools,
because they often give fresh perspective and breath to passages which
have lost their impact due to familiarity or because they are difficult
passages. In fact, the Message translation would have been helpful to
me as a child who often read and even memorized Psalm 23. The first

phrase, "The Lord is my shepherd; I shall not want," always confused me because I was too young to even notice the semicolon. I could not understand, 1) why I should not want Jesus to be my shepherd, and 2) why it was ok to say that at church!

A good paraphrase, like the Message or the Living Bible, is like butter. It adds flavor and fun to a good meal, but too much of it causes problems. Just as it would be absurd to have butter as the main course of a meal, it is not a good idea to use a paraphrase as a main translation for devotional reading, study, or teaching.

A good translation is an important tool for studying the Bible. Invest the time to find an accurate translation you can understand, and learn about the strengths and weaknesses of your primary translation and other translations you reference. Use other translations to strengthen your study and understanding of Scripture, and even consider using a paraphrase occasionally.

APPENDIX 2: THE DANGER OF ALLEGORIZING PASSAGES

Many people approach the Bible as if it has a secret, encoded message that only a few people can understand. Many pastors promote this type of thinking by the way they teach and preach the Bible, finding metaphorical meanings which are not the plain meaning of the text and are often not even a secondary meaning of the text.

Let me illustrate. I once heard a sermon based on the following passage from Matthew 27:57-60:

> *"When it was evening, there came a rich man from Arimathea, named Joseph, who also was a disciple of Jesus. He went to Pilate and asked for the body of Jesus. Then Pilate ordered it to be given to him. And Joseph took the body and wrapped it in a clean linen shroud and laid it in his own new tomb, which he had cut in the rock. And he rolled a great stone to the entrance of the tomb and went away."*

This passage records the moments after Jesus' death on the cross when Joseph of Arimathea took Jesus' body and placed it in a tomb. In the sermon I heard from this passage, everything had a symbolic meaning.

| Allegorical Interpretation of Matthew 27:57-60 ||
Element of the Passage	Symbolic Meaning
Jesus' Body	The Local Church (Body of Christ)
Joseph	Local Pastors and Missionaries
Asking for the Body of Jesus	Praying for God to Build the Church
Wrapping the Body in Linen	Keeping the Church Pure
Cutting a Tomb from Rock	Hard Work Required to Build a Church

Sermons like this, called allegorical sermons, are very common. I'd bet (though I'm not a betting man!) that most of you have heard a sermon about David and Goliath in which Goliath represented the giants in your life like financial problems, depression, disease, etc., and you were encouraged to trust God to deliver you. I've heard that sermon—I've preached that sermon! But I would not preach it again. That's an allegorical interpretation, which makes it an invalid interpretation. Isn't God powerful enough to defeat any giant I might face in my life? Isn't it true that local pastors and missionaries should pray, work hard, and keep the local church pure? Of course those things are true, BUT, that's not what those passages are teaching.

Alternative Allegorical Interpretation of Matthew 27:57-61	
Element of the Passage	**Symbolic Meaning**
Jesus' Body	The Local Church (Body of Christ)
Joseph	Local Pastors and Missionaries
Pilate	Local Government Officials
Asking for the Body of Jesus	Asking Local Governments for Permission to Take the Church out of Society and Live Separately
Wrapping the Body in Linen	Keeping the Church Pure
Cutting a Tomb from Rock	Hard Work Required to Prepare a Place for the Church to Live Separately
Laying the Body in the Tomb	Leading the Church to the Separate Place
Rolling a Stone in Front of the Entrance	Sealing the Church Off from the Rest of the World

When pastors and Bible teachers interpret and teach allegorical interpretations of passages, two things happen. First, they open themselves up to error because they teach their ideas instead of what the passage actually says. For instance, using the same passage from Matthew 27, let's imagine a different allegory that actually fits the details of the story more accurately but would lead us into error.

I can hear the preacher now, "Church, if we really want to experience resurrection and new life, we must shut ourselves off from the rest of the world and wait on God to do His work!" Interesting allegory. Horrible missiology. Bad sermon.

Let me be crystal clear—I do not believe either of these allegorical interpretations of Matthew 27:57-61 are correct. The alternate allegorical interpretation simply serves to show how allegorical interpretations are nothing more than the conjectures of the interpreter and how they can lead to really bad doctrine like leading the church to shut itself off from the world. However, that's not all that lessons and sermons based on allegorical interpretations do. Second, they also present the task of proper interpretation of Bible passages as something only a few people can do. How difficult would it be to understand the Bible if every story had two meanings—one that was the plain, straightforward meaning and another that was allegorical, mystical, and only accessible to a handful of very gifted people?

Don't Forget the Reformation

As we approach the 500th anniversary of the beginning of the Protestant Reformation, let's take a moment to remember why and how the doctrine and practice of the church had become so corrupt and full of errors. One of the foundational issues—arguably *the* foundational issue—which led to the dark times just before the Reformation was that no one had a copy of the Bible in a language they could understand. In other words, no one knew what the Bible actually said. People were left to trust the local priest to tell them not only what the Bible meant, but what it actually said. Furthermore, many of the priests, not fluent in Latin (the language of virtually all Bibles at the time), didn't even know what the Bible said and trusted in the interpretations of the more gifted officials of the church. Dr. Steve Lawson describes the situation in England this way,

> "England lay covered under a dark night of spiritual darkness. The church in England remained shrouded in the midnight of

spiritual ignorance. The knowledge of Scriptures had been all but extinguished in the land. Although there were some twenty thousand priests in England, it was said that they could not so much as translate into English a simple clause from the Lord's Prayer. The clergy were so bogged down in a mire of religious superstition that they had no knowledge of the truth . . .translating the Bible into English was considered a capital crime."[23]

One of the fiercest battles of the Reformation was the battle to get the Bible translated into the languages of the people and distributed across Europe. Many people gave their lives for this cause, and it was that cause, which spread the fires of the Reformation more than any other.

The New Priests

Now, 500 years later, there is a new but related danger in the Western world. Despite access to the Bible on a scale unimaginable to previous generations, most people, and even most Christians who faithful attend local churches don't understand biblical doctrine. In my opinion, the problem begins in the pulpit. Pastors who use allegorical preaching methods indirectly communicate to their people that the Bible's message is encoded with symbols which the average person could never understand. That message has been communicated so consistently that many people have given up trying to understand the Bible through personal study, and they just show up to church expecting the pastor to share the real meaning of the Bible. In other words, the Bible might as well be written in Latin! Furthermore, many pastors, although they might not admit it, are like those 15th and 16th century priests who did not know Latin and therefore could not read or properly interpret Bible passages. Many modern pastors feel inadequate to interpret the Bible because their allegories aren't as sharp as allegories they hear from others. That's why many preachers simply parrot what they hear from other pastors.

Perhaps you feel like that. Maybe you think, "I could never know what that passage actually means, so I better leave that to the 'experts.'" Let

---

[23]. Lawson, Steven J. *The Daring Mission of William Tyndale*. Orlando, FL: Reformation Trust Publishing, 2015, xviii

me be clear—there is a place for expert scholars who dedicate their lives to understanding the message of the Bible, and there is a place for local pastors who take the meaning of a text and apply it to the local situation, but equally important is the role of the non-pastor, non-scholar who studies the Word to keep the pastors and scholars in check. Acts describes the people of Berea this way, *"They received the word with all eagerness, examining the Scriptures daily to see if these things were so"* Acts 17:11.

APPENDIX 3: THE HISTORY OF INTERPRETATION

What's the history of interpretation? I'm glad you asked! Since the late centuries of the era before Jesus, Jewish and then Christian religious scholars have studied and discussed Scripture, and the results of that process have produced a standard interpretation of passages, which has the best chance of being accurate. While it may seem to some observers outside of the world of Christian scholarship that no one can agree on the meaning of Bible passages—after all, that's why we have so many denominations, right?—the truth is that there is an incredibly high degree of agreement among scholars about the meaning of most passages in the Bible. By my estimate, the passages that produce heated debates among evangelical Bible students and result in doctrinal differences represent less than 5% of the Biblical text.

Biblical interpretation is like open source software. It's accessible to so many technicians that eventually any problems which arise will be solved by a group in the community, and over time, the rest of the community will come to accept the work of those technicians. Not into programing? Then think about it this way—the Grand Canyon records the history of the path of the Colorado River, and the bottom of the canyon contains the path into which the river eventually settled. The history of biblical interpretation records many variant interpretations, but over time, those interpretations not supported by clear and compelling evidence have dried up, leaving a majority interpretation. There are certainly competing channels and countless tributaries, but there is more common understanding and interpretation than is often perceived by those outside the world of biblical scholarship.

Let me give two examples, one from each of the major splits in church history. First, in the Great Schism of 1054 AD, the Eastern Church and Western Church split over the interpretation of Acts 2:33 and similar verses. The verse reads, "Being therefore exalted at the right hand of God, and having received from the Father the promise of the Holy Spirit, he has poured out this that you yourselves are seeing and hearing." The Eastern Church holds that this verse and other verses like it teach that the Holy Spirit proceeds forth from (comes from) the Father, but not the Son. The Western Church, however, interprets this verse and others to teach that the Holy Spirit proceeds forth from the Father and the Son. Second, during the Protestant Reformation, two of the great reformers, John Calvin and Martin Luther, considered joining their independent movements into one single movement. As they discussed the issues, they found agreement on all but one point—the interpretation of Jesus' words in Luke 22:19-20 in which He compares the bread and wine of the Lord's Supper to His body and blood. Luther believed that Christ was spiritually present in the bread and wine, while Calvin believed the bread and wine were only symbols of Jesus' body and blood.

Those who study church history learn that disagreements are often over small details of texts, which lead to competing doctrines. That's not to say that such disagreements are inconsequential or that we should put them all aside and pursue ecumenism (the reuniting of the denominations of the church in spite of serious doctrinal disagreements). I'm simply making the point that major doctrinal and denominational disagreements are not evidence that we have no hope of properly interpreting the Bible. The history of the church stands in stark contrast to that conclusion. With overwhelming agreement on most passages, the church has established a history of interpretation that those who hope to study the Bible would be wise to use. We can stand on the shoulders of giants if we so choose.

www.ingramcontent.com/pod-product-compliance
Lightning Source LLC
Chambersburg PA
CBHW022013090426
42741CB00007B/1014